# JOURNEY TO THE EAST

*Jeanneret in Athens, September 1911, as sketched by his friend Auguste Klipstein (courtesy FLC)*

# JOURNEY TO THE EAST

Le Corbusier
(Charles-Edouard Jeanneret)

Edited and annotated by Ivan Žaknić
Translated by Ivan Žaknić
in collaboration with Nicole Pertuiset

The MIT Press
Cambridge, Massachusetts
London, England

# CONTENTS

For CIP data and copyright information, see page 270.

# ACKNOWLEDGMENTS

In bringing this book to publication, I have been privileged to work with many different people and material from many sources.

First and foremost, I would like to express my deep gratitude to the late Héléna Strassova, literary agent for Le Corbusier's works, who passed away in January 1980 in Paris, as I was working on this manuscript.

I would also like to thank the people of La Fondation Le Corbusier in Paris, for their kind assistance in making the many drawings and documents from their collection available for my research and inspection. In particular I thank André Wogenscky, the president at the time, for kindly permitting the publication of some selected drawings; Madame Evelyn Trehin, Délégué-Général, for her willingness to help—and often at very short notice—during my visits to Paris; and Pierre Bourlier for making the material available.

In doing research on this book, kind assistance was provided by Fernand Donzé, director, and Hélène Augsburger, librarian, at the Bibliothèque de La Chaux-de-Fonds, where I was able to consult the original manuscripts and drawings by Jeanneret from the 1911 journey, donated to the library by L'Eplattenier's and Ritter's heirs.

Also my thanks to the Swiss National Library in Bern for making available to me the Jeanneret-Ritter correspondence.

I am indebted to Jean Petit, the editor of the French publication of *Le Voyage d'Orient* (1966), for his advice and kind permission to reproduce here several drawings which date from this journey and appeared in his book *Le Corbusier Lui Même*.

In translating and editing *Le Voyage d'Orient,* many have helped, and the list would not be complete without a word of thanks to all who at different levels and in different areas contributed: Jean Pierre Cauvin, Douglas Hickman, Donna Rogers, Carolyn Czichos at the University of Texas, where I was teaching at the time. Very special appreciation to the acting chairman of the School of Architecture at Cornell University, Henry Richardson, for lightening my teaching load that I might bring this work to its successful completion.

I am indebted to my original reader, Gunesh Gery.

A very special place is occupied by John Gery, a poet and longtime friend, whose mark is felt throughout, and my wife Caryl, my support and inspiration.

Tanis Furst typed the final manuscript with the utmost skill and patience.

Lastly, I am very grateful to Kenneth Frampton, whose support for this work came at the crucial time, and Nicole Pertuiset, who contributed so generously to the final shape of the text.

Ivan Žaknić

# EDITOR'S PREFACE

Fifty-five years separated the writing of *Le Voyage d'Orient* (Journey to the East) and its publication in book form by Forces Vives, Paris, in 1966. It is the first book that the young Charles-Edouard Jeanneret (Le Corbusier) wrote and the last he submitted for publication, only a few weeks before his death on August 27, 1965.

For us this book bears witness to some of his most influential discoveries and his first attempts to capture his impressions and observations. It is written with an enthusiasm he never lost, even in his maturity as other more important challenges set in during his long and fruitful career as architect, urbanist, painter, and writer.

The long interval between the writing and publication of this work might raise questions about its merit as a literary achievement, further reinforced by Jeanneret's own reluctance to publish it after two unsuccessful attempts in 1912 and 1914. Perhaps Le Corbusier intended the book to be his unprefaced last confession.

Written initially as a travel journal for his friends in La Chaux-de-Fonds, the first half of these notes was serialized in the newspaper *La Feuille d'Avis* during 1911, while Jeanneret was still traveling. Before embarking on this journey, Jeanneret had carefully premeditated his choice of a local newspaper from among the five published in La Chaux-de-Fonds at the time. He consulted his teacher and mentor, Charles L'Eplattenier, for advice concerning the choice and the possibility of obtaining remuneration for his efforts. Through L'Eplattenier's influence not only were Jeanneret's articles accepted, but he even negotiated a payment of one sou per line.

The collection of impressions, observations, and letters to his friends in the first half of the book constitute the material serialized in *La Feuille d'Avis*. The chapter "In the West" was added to the manuscript in 1912 when Jeanneret first attempted to publish it as a book.

It was then, through the mediation of his close friend William Ritter, an influential writer and artist of French-speaking Switzerland, that the thirty-one-page typed manuscript was submitted to Mercure de France in Paris, a publisher of several of Ritter's books. Mercure de France returned the manuscript to Ritter in Munich on December 23, 1912, but the reasons for its return and rejection are not known.

A second attempt by Jeanneret to publish the manuscript followed in 1914; this time he included two additional chapters on Mount Athos and the Parthenon. In the original manuscript the chapter on Mount Athos was entitled "Souvenirs—l'Athos" (Recollections of Athos), not simply "Athos," as it was published in *Le Voyage d'Orient* (1966); this has caused some confusion about the true date of its composition. The authentic title has been restored in this English language edition. The chapter on the Parthenon remains virtually unchanged, except for a few minor omissions which are provided in the editor's footnotes. Both the typed thirty-one-page manuscript and the handwritten originals of the Athos and Parthenon chapters were in Ritter's possession, and only after his death were they donated to the Bibliothèque de La Chaux-de-Fonds by his adopted son Josef Ritter-Tcherv. During my visits there I was able to examine both manuscripts.

Evidence also indicates that Jeanneret contemplated publishing the work once again, near the end of World War I, in a series of books to be undertaken in collaboration with Amédée Ozenfant. This collection was to be known as "Les Commentaires sur l'Art et la Vie Moderne" and was to include an illustrated version of *Le Voyage d'Orient* with the projected title of "Tilleul et Camomile."

When I began this translation, there was, in addition to the French version of *Le Voyage d'Orient* (Forces Vives, 1966), only one other publication that featured parts of this book. *L'Almanach d'Architecture*

*Moderne* in Paris, 1925, published excerpts from three chapters, under the heading "Carnet de Route, 1910." These included parts of "Les Mosques," illustrated with Corbusier's own drawings from the journey; parts of "Sur l'Acropole" illustrated with photographs by Frederich Boissonas, and almost the entire text of "En Occident," which contained several instances of national and cultural stereotyping later suppressed for the 1966 publication.

Soon I felt the need to investigate the many questions raised by these multiple texts, to clarify allusions, and to correct misassumptions, wrong dates, and typographical errors. To gain familiarity with locations described in the text and greater confidence in my translation, I traveled to many locations on Jeanneret's itinerary, including Vienna, Belgrade, Istanbul, Athens, Delphi, Naples, Pompeii, Rome, Florence, Lucerne, and La Chaux-de-Fonds. *Journey to the East* was thus for me an experiment not only in research, style, and method of writing but also in travel, through which I discovered the world that so deeply affected the twenty-four-year-old Jeanneret. Wherever I judge it important, I have footnoted names and places not always as obvious to the English reader of today as they may have been to Jeanneret's small circle of friends in La Chaux-de-Fonds in 1911, or to those who traveled similar paths through the Balkans and Istanbul, Athos, and Athens before World War I.

In addition to the 1966 text, I consulted the newspaper articles that were published in 1911. The private correspondences between Jeanneret and his two friends and mentors, Charles L'Eplattenier and William Ritter, were extremely helpful in providing more intimate insight into the personality of these two people who were so influential on the young Jeanneret.

From the outset I recognized the importance of familiarizing myself with the numerous drawings from this journey which, needless to say, were for Jeanneret a more fluent medium for capturing images than was the written word. Some of these drawings have been lost, many are undated or inaccurately dated, some have never been published before, and some were published over the years by Jeanneret and other authors in various articles and books not always relating to this period or this journey. To support and lend graphic vividness to the text, a selection of previously published and unpublished illustrations has been assembled here, in their proper place.

Only one chapter from this translation, "The Mosques," has been published to date, in *Oppositions* 18 (Fall 1979). It is accompanied by a short interpretive essay, "Of Le Corbusier's Eastern Journey."

To English-speaking readers, even those previously acquainted with Jeanneret's writing, some of the passages of *Journey to the East* will seem a little confused and confusing. Where it seemed useful, I have added footnotes to clarify, correct, and explain places visited, references made, or views expressed. Although Jeanneret himself suppressed some of the naively autobiographical sections during his attempts to publish the travelogue in book form, some examples still remain. The text translated here is complete; all ellipses are in the original.

It is clear that Jeanneret at the time of *Le Voyage* had not yet found his true subject. He does not return to his early drafts to bring us happier literary results, a finished product rather than preliminary sketches. This was his first attempt to write for potential publication, and he did it at full speed as he moved from city to city, place to place, by boat, train, horse, and carriage, all the while devouring the experiences. We cannot but assume that there was much he wanted to say, so much he wanted to see, that he was not to miss anything except—perhaps—punctuation, direct objects, and, at times, subjects. We feast upon an abundance of adjectives. In these travel notes Jeanneret admits to his inability to cope with the overwhelming impact of the experiences he lived through and confesses to his own incapacity in his native language. "These notes are lifeless; the beauties I have seen always break down under my pen. . . ." Despite these self-deprecating words, Le Corbusier reveals himself as a well-prepared and mature student. His views were still very much affected by the books he read in preparation for this journey. Some of the books he carried with him. Occasionally he referred to them; at other times he was inspired by them in his own writing. A close reading reveals his indebtedness to Claude Ferrer's *L'Homme Qui Assassina,* for example, in the chapter about the Istanbul bazaar, and to Ernest Renan's "La Priere sur l'Acropole" for the dramatic presentation of the Parthenon.

This was not the same Grand Tour made famous by other nineteenth-century men of letters such as Lord Byron, who traveled not only with trunks full of books but also with servants, valets, interpreters, several beds, camping equipment, and English saddles and bridles. Jeanneret, with his backpack and one companion, rides second class on ships and packed trains, on top of mules and donkeys, and most often on foot. His other companions are bedbugs, not the Countess Guiccioli. He is not a *cavalier servente* but a *giaour* who admires the beauty of Turkish women through their veils and becomes ecstatic when one of them, one day, addresses him with the "Sprechen Sie Deutsch . . . Guten Tag, mein Herr!" and then disappears into the crowd with her governess.

Unlike Lord Byron, Jeanneret did not scratch his name on any temple to mark his presence, but he tried to unlock their mystery. He did carry a camera and took many photographs. He placed little value on their usefulness, however, much preferring his *carnets* filled with sketches. Of this process and experience he later wrote, in *Creation Is a Patient Search* (trans. James Palmes):

*When one travels and works with visual things—architecture, painting or sculpture—one uses one's eyes and draws, so as to fix deep down in one's experience what is seen. Once the impression has been recorded by the pencil, it stays for good, entered, registered, inscribed. The camera is a tool for idlers, who use a machine to do their seeing for them. To draw oneself, to trace the lines, handle the volumes, organize the surface . . . all this means first to look, and then to observe and finally perhaps to discover . . . and it is then that inspiration may come. Inventing, creating, one's whole being is drawn into action, and it is this action which counts. Others stood indifferent—but you saw!*

The travels to the East opened wide horizons for Jeanneret and exposed him to an immense new social and visual culture. Jeanneret was above all a visual person, and he does not hesitate to tell the story in penetrating images that rush to be absorbed and recorded. Jeanneret's writing at this time contains much poetry, and many concepts that were to make him a twentieth-century polemicist par excellence.

By the time that he wrote *Towards a New Architecture*, Le Corbusier, though still as emotionally involved in those experiences as ever, was capable of sublimating the romance of his first exposure to them. The Parthenon remained for him the measure of all art and architecture, the divine ideal and the absolute master. Of the Acropolis, upon which he spent six weeks observing and sketching, he later wrote in the third person in *Creation Is a Patient Search*:

*The columns of the North facade and the architrave of the Parthenon were still lying on the ground. Touching them with his fingers, caressing them, he grasps the proportions of the design. Amazement: reality has nothing in common with books of instruction. Here everything was a shout of inspiration, a dance in the sunlight . . . and a final and supreme warning: do not believe until you have seen and measured . . . and touched with your own fingers.*

There was, it seems, a pre-Parthenon Jeanneret and a post-Parthenon Le Corbusier. It was after the experience of Mount Athos and the Parthenon that he decided to be an architect, and he confesses it here: "How painful was the ecstasy that seized us in those temples of the East! How withdrawn I felt, overcome by shame. Yet the hours spent in those silent sanctuaries inspired in me a youthful courage and the true desire to become an honorable builder."

Ivan Žaknić

# PREFACE TO THE FRENCH EDITION

In 1911 Charles-Edouard Jeanneret, a draftsman in the office of Peter Behrens in Berlin, decided with his friend, Auguste Klipstein, to undertake a journey whose destination was Constantinople. From May to October, with very little money, the two friends toured Bohemia, Serbia, Rumania, Bulgaria, and Turkey.

It was then that Charles-Edouard Jeanneret discovered architecture: a magnificent play of forms in light, a coherent system of the mind.

During this journey from Dresden to Constantinople, and from Athens to Pompeii, Charles-Edouard Jeanneret kept a travel diary. In it he noted his impressions, and he also executed a great number of drawings which taught him to observe and to see.

From these notes he extracted articles, some of which were to be published by *La Feuille d'Avis* of La Chaux-de-Fonds. Later he would reassemble and complete these manuscripts to form a book. The book, *Le Voyage d'Orient,* was to be published by Gaspard Valette of Mercure de France in 1914. However, the war prevented that publication, and the manuscript was stored among the archives of Le Corbusier. Fifty-four years after his journey, he decided at long last to publish the book that is a testimony to his wonderment and discoveries as a young man. In July 1965 he edited the manuscript and annotated it meticulously, relying on nothing more than his memory.

Here then is *Journey to the East,* considered by Le Corbusier to be an important and revealing document on the most decisive year of his growth as an artist and as an architect.

# JOURNEY TO THE EAST

# ITINERARY OF THE
# JOURNEY TO THE EAST, 1911

Berlin, Dresden, Prague, Vienna, Vác, Budapest, Baja, Belgrade, Niš, Knjaževac, [Negotin], Giurgiu, Bucharest, Tŭrnovo, Gabrovo, Shipka, Kazanlŭk, [Stara Zagora], Adrianople (Erdine), Rodosto (Tekirdağ), Constantinople (Istanbul), Bursa, Daphni, Athos, Salonika, Athens, Itea, Delphi, Patras, Brindisi, Naples, Pompeii, Rome, Florence, Lucerne, [La Chaux-de-Fonds]. (The cities in brackets are mentioned by Jeanneret in the text but were omitted in the French edition.)

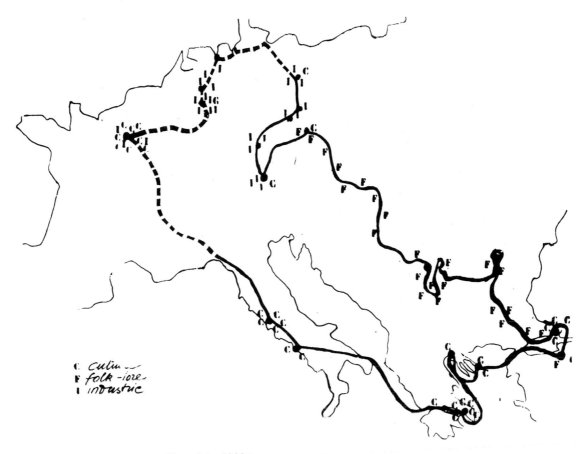

C culin...
F folk-lore.
I industrie

*Map of the 1911 journey,
also showing Jeanneret's
trips to Italy, 1907, Paris,
1908, Germany, 1910*

# TO MY BROTHER,
# THE MUSICIAN ALBERT JEANNERET

Surely you know how I wish this piece that I am dedicating to you were better! But I have nothing else. You know only too well how much these lines—written for an audience who really didn't want them—have tarnished the joy and disturbed the serenity with which everything there filled me. I give them to you simply now to give you something, because I feel like giving you something today.

Your face made the journey from the beginning to the end—through the Danube, Stamboul, Athens, but was mislaid, unknown to me, among old papers. It had your features but not exactly. I sketched it, unbeknown to you, at the Wald-Schenke in Hellerau during the Christmas of 1910: you were devouring slices of blood sausage on buttered bread (one of those menus forced on us by our pocketbooks in that country!)[1] The voracious way you were eating that sausage and butter disgusted me. At certain times, and precisely at that moment, you struck me as incredibly gluttonous.

That sketch was a form of protest. This is how I pictured you, and how I think of you. Perhaps, in fact, you are even delighted with it.

The other day they told me about the conviction with which you defended my French, during your stay here this summer—my very poor, sad, incompetent French; for me as a draftsman it remained my only means of expression during those moments when my emotions got the better of me. They quoted you an unintelligible sentence, the kind of monster that the typographer of *La Feuille d'Avis* knew how to set up, and also the kind tolerated by "our family friend," the publisher of that paper. You replied that it was perfect, perfect, perfect, and that you didn't want to hear any more about it.

So, my dear old brother, we have been helping each other for years.

We won't stop, will we? Amid the fluctuating esteem of even our closest friends—for they cannot entirely escape the sway of public opinion—may our affection remain firm, constant, absolute—like that distant horizon, between Limnos and the Aegean.

# A FEW IMPRESSIONS[1]

—To travel from country to country for so many months, remarked two charming acquaintances, the other day in Berlin—won't you lose your sense of appreciation, dull your enthusiasm, so that you no longer see things except with a somewhat disillusioned eye? At times, as during our last talks together, your unexpected judgments really astonished us! . . . You are leaving right away for the East; we suppose your intentions are not to miss anything the road has to offer, on either side. . . .

—Such impressions, and varied and numerous! . . . Our concern justifies itself. Don't hold it against us.

It turned out true, after all: under the heavy vaults of the Tiergarten during our late strolls along the glaucous canals of the Spree, or while returning from a killing excursion into the stony maze of old or new cities of *Germania,* it happened that I disapproved of some revered dome; that I crowned that famous city lying at the mouth of a river on a plain and dominated by an unduly romantic Burg with a question mark; that I railed against some other many-sided medieval eyesore flanked with a frame of donjons, ditches, and crenelated walls, and against its equivocal smile beneath its epical helmet which was completely slashed by black factory chimneys and blotched by leprous filthy and stinking fumes.

Against this ever more theatrical sight, I contrasted another, somewhat less fashionable, because fortunately less known: a serene smile under a blue sky, all around sculpted stones and carefully stuccoed amid golden wheat and bursting red flowers, where the blue sky is intensified by the deep-set stars.

I had spoken with enthusiasm about some modern works and had finally passed judgment on medieval Germany in favor of the sober

*Frankfurt, April 1911 (courtesy FLC). One of thirteen watercolors exhibited under the title "Langage de Pierre" in Munich (1911), Neuchâtel (1912), Zurich (1913), and Paris (at the Salon d'Automne, 1913)*

works of a hundred or two hundred years ago. The foolish romanticism, so little expressive of our intelligence, exasperated me. Admiration had become dampened time and again; as if beside a raging river, for instance, submerged between jagged, rough red rocks, but further on spread out like a living god upon a plain blessed by its presence, the foul taste of gable and tower builders had left the junk heap effects of a ruffian.

At certain times the great avenues smothered in greenery, paved with an asphalt so polished by passing cars that the setting sun reflected in an infinite line of fire through myriad black columns of trees, had appeared to me exalting creations. And the sordid alleys around the tastelessly restored domes, buried beneath the excessive corbelling of neglected facades, the stenches that stagnate there, the shady people who lurk there, and the teeming bands of whining children, many times made me flee . . . whereas Baedeker swooned and, to show his joy, plucked stars from the sky and turned them into single, double, or triple laudatory asterisks.[2] Thus I abused the once proud ladies of the manor, ridiculed fat "old beaux" and browbeat too many nineteenth-century parvenus. Names—very handsome names—I sullied them. Wretched names, wretched magic of words that I am blighting! Un-worthy sacrifice!

To be forgiven, I had to explain myself.

—To begin with, I ventured, there are the overrated reputations. In the world of art, elbowed often by the world of fashion, there are the monopolizers and the bluffers. Here one also meets the modest and the timid. Opposed to noisy protesters are the serenely oblivious.

—Besides, young ladies, you should recognize that in the eyes of others, an art lover always has his head slightly askew in spite of himself and remember that I, for example, have an uncle who is hopelessly convinced that I make unfair judgments for the sole purpose of opposing popular opinion.

—In short, if for me beauty appears to consist above all of harmony and not of size, bulk, height, or the expense or theatrical glamor, I add to this mode of seeing, my mode of being. I am young—an ephemeral sin—I am consequently prone to rash judgments. I admire eclecticism, but I'll wait until I am white-haired before accepting it blindly. On the contrary, I open my eyes very wide, taking in all around me, my myopic eyes behind my glasses—these sorry spectacles that bestow upon me a doctoral air or the look of a clergyman. I am talking a lot of nonsense. Much worse, to the great disapproval of those close to me, I bring myself to change my attitude and contradict myself more often than is seemly. Thus, when I am in a bad mood, I snort; whereas at other times, my inquisitive young ladies, I feel myself being profoundly moved, drifting through a reverie to the rhythm of subjugating scherzos, entirely overcome by the grand Harmony!

No, you skeptical young ladies, one doesn't become jaded by traveling. One only becomes a little aristocratic in one's preferences, and, upon my word, that's all for the better these days when everything is becoming socialized, and especially so for a reader of *La Sentinelle*.[3] This journey to the East, far from the gossamer architecture of the north, is a response to the persistent call of the sun, the wide expanses of blue seas and the great white walls of temples—Constantinople, Asia Minor, Greece, southern Italy—will be like an ideally shaped vase from which the heart's most profound feelings will flow . . .

This is how at two o'clock in the morning on the white ship floating down the immense river between Budapest and Belgrade, I cannot put a stop to them, forgetting to go on deck to watch the full moon ascend through a labyrinth of stars!

*Four views of the Royal Palace (now the Hradčany Presidential Palace) in Prague, sketched by Jean- neret for his friend and mentor, William Ritter,* *who advised him to include Prague in his itinerary (courtesy Bibliothèque de La Chaux-de-Fonds)*

# A LETTER TO FRIENDS[1]

at the "Ateliers d'Art" in La-Chaux-de-Fonds[2]

My dear old Perrin, greetings!

If Octave at his rue de la Sorbonne place in Paris were reading this respectable, much too charitable, journal, I would already have received his condolences in vivid language and framed in black, because this child is not doing too well and is ready to die even before being born! I have undertaken to write accounts of my travels—practically a journal! But I am the unhappiest of men: for it is, you must admit, the utmost tedium; and the thought of spoiling the siesta of so many acquaintances distresses me. So I come to you. You like forms (indeed, plastic arts) almost as much as Georges, and you are aware of the beauty of a sphere. I come to you to talk about vases—peasant vases, traditional pottery. Incidentally, I shall comment on several ports along my route, so my editor will be content. Marius Perrenond, our potter from the Atelier, deserved, it may seem to you, this "ceramicological" epistle; but Marius does not yet like the sphere enough: so then to you some trifles on contours and my ecstasies.

You recognize these joys: to feel the generous belly of a vase, to caress its slender neck, and then to explore the subtleties of its contours. To thrust your hands into the deepest part of your pockets and, with your eyes half-closed, to give way slowly to the intoxication of the fantastic glazes, the burst of yellows, the velvet tone of the blues; to be involved in the animated fight between brutal black masses and victorious white elements. You will understand this even better if you imagine, after the tiring months of travel, my somewhat stylish studio turned blue by cigarette smoke, and sunk in armchairs or lying on couches, you and our friends, whom I will see again after so many years and to whom I will do the favor of stories that could put alarm clocks to sleep! The vases about which I am now going to tell you will be there, bulging mightily.

I would have you know that, since Budapest, we have secured an arsenal of pot-bellies and bottlenecks capable of summoning up those unforgettable hours. In our travels we passed through countries where the artist peasant matches with authority the color to the line and the line to the form, and we were green with envy! But this continued without end! Even under torrential rains, which made Auguste, the companion of my miseries, groan until finally we descended into the "Alibabesque" grottos. And then, be it in a dingy shop or in a poor underground cavern in Budapest, or even in an attic caked with dowager dust, at the torrid noon hour in a village on the Hungarian plain, it was unrestrained debauchery. Can you feel it? The jars being there, in their joyous dazzle and robust strength, and their beauty was comforting. To unearth them, we had to make a search through all the sad, international, and rootless bric-a-brac that inundates all of Europe: and still, even here in Hungary where the peasant knows how to create like a great artist, we found the offerings of the merchants most humiliating, and the sway of fashion over souls still naive, a most disastrous effect. There was too much multicolored glassware with golden floral designs, too much china spotted with the shameful ornamentation of Louis XV seashells, or with flowerets dressed in the taste of the recent past. We had to flee from the invading and dirty "Europeanization" to the tranquil refuges where—abating, and soon to be submerged—the great popular tradition survives.

The art of the peasant is a striking creation of aesthetic sensuality. If art elevates itself above the sciences, it is precisely because, in opposition to them, it stimulates sensuality and awakens profound echoes in the physical being. It gives to the body—to the animal—its fair share, and then upon this healthy base, conducive to the expansion of joy, it knows how to erect the most noble of pillars.

Thus this traditional art, like a lingering warm caress, embraces the entire land, covering it with the same flowers that unite or mingle races, climates, and places. It has spread out without constraint, with the spiritedness of a beautiful animal. The forms are voluminous and swollen with vitality, the line continually unites and mingles native scenes, or offers, right alongside and on the same object, the magic of geometry: an astonishing union of fundamental instincts and of those susceptible to more abstract speculations.

The color, it too is not descriptive but evocative—always symbolic. It is the end and not the means. It exists for the caress and for the intoxication of the eye, and as such, paradoxically, with a hearty laugh it jostles the great inhibited giants, even the Giottos, even the Grecos, the Cézannes and the Van Goghs!

Considered from a certain point of view, folk art outlives the highest of civilizations. It remains a norm, a sort of measure whose standard is man's ancestor—the savage, if you will.

I'm already boring you, my friend Perrin, yet these potteries from Hungary and Serbia would suffice for endless chats, since they could encompass the study of anonymous and traditional art.

Let me recall these two things which struck us during our visit to the potters on the Hungarian plains and in the Serbian Balkans, and to give you a rest, and to make you envious, I will describe for you some of the villages on the Danube.

First and foremost among these men who do not reason is the instinctive appreciation for the *organic line,* born from the correlation between the most utilitarian line and that which encloses the most expansive volume—thus the most beautiful.

—Beauty, Mr. Grasset told me one day in Paris, It is joy.[3]

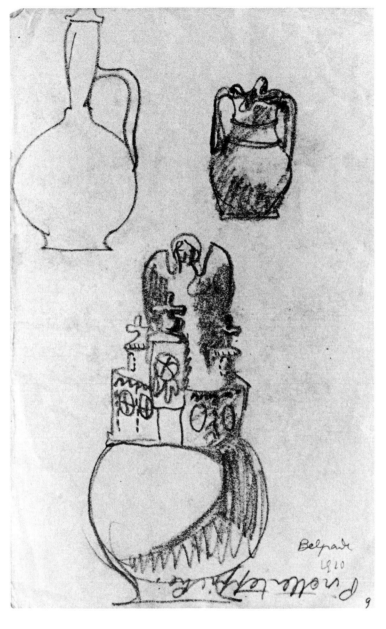

*Pottery from the Balkans (courtesy FLC)*

—Why, he added, should one copy some shriveled bud? That's monstrous!

Joy—it is a tree spread out like a magnificent palm, with flowers and with all its fruits. Beauty is this splendid flourish of youth.

In effect these pots too are young, beaming—allow me these adjectives—with their curves expanding to the bursting point, and what a contrast they make, created as they are on the wheel of the village potter, whose simple mind probably doesn't wander farther than that of his neighbor the grocer's but whose fingers unconsciously obey the rules of an age-old tradition, in contrast to those forms of a disturbing fantasy, or a stupefying imbecility, conceived by who knows whom in the unknown corners of large modern factories; those are nothing but the foolish whims of some low-ranking draftsman who draws such form for the sole purpose of differentiating it from the one that he drew yesterday. We continued to discover along the Danube, and later in Adrianople, exactly these forms, which the Mycenaean painters covered with black arabesques; what a dogged adherence to the beaten track! But then, there is nothing I know more lamentable than this mania of today to disown tradition for the sole purpose of creating the coveted "new." This deviation from the creative forces is reflected in every domain of art, and it not only procures us impractical teapots, ugly cups, shabby flowerpots with inverted contours, but also dangerous chairs and badly designed chests, and houses with unpardonably bizarre, heteroclite, and absurd silhouettes,—O my dear sculptor! The litter of useless sculptures and their tactlessness. We live, don't we, in an environment that is not livable—disorganized—*de-organized* . . .

I will go further and tell you in two words something both exciting and distressing: these potters "don't give a damn" about their own art. Their fingers do the work, not their minds or their hearts. Their mouths drop in amazement when we enter their shops and make a clean sweep. And be sure that out of their products—nowadays diversified—they offer us precisely the bad ones, glittering in sometimes revolting taste, good imitations of trifles that they glimpsed one day on the market stall of the peddler from the big city. Their own art is no more than a surviving relic, and, if in a few years you go through Knjaževac in the Balkans, for example, you will find not one of these pieces which I will show you upon my return: they were already twenty years old when we unearthed them from the rubbish in which these "sins" of youth collect dust.

Considering this, Auguste, who is preparing for his doctorate in art history, suddenly felt overwhelmed by the birth of a revelatory theory. He had perceived this ultimate crisis evident in the pottery of Hungary and Serbia, and, envisaging in one stroke all the arts and all the epochs, he formulated the theory of "The psychological moment in popular pottery in the twentieth-century arts." In German it sounds much better: "Der psychologische Moment, etc." Auguste, I swear to you, never was able to finish it. Nor could I have helped him. And thus, with this second child, also not doing too well, dead before having seen daylight, and which to Auguste will be worth Octave's condolences, framed in black and in a Vedic language, I am going to tell you to what exquisite nests our madness carried us.[4]

It was Wednesday morning, June 7th. The great white boat had left Budapest at nightfall. Helped by the strong current, it made its way down the immense watercourse that marked out with a black path to the right and the left the two distant riverbanks, which join at the horizon in their interminable flight. Almost everyone was asleep: the privileged on the red velvet benches in the first-class smoking room, the peasants, men and women here and there with innumerable bundles often adorned with crude and gay embroideries. In the open expanse of the sky the moon dimmed the starlight. I knew nothing about the countries we were passing through because no one ever talks about them. Yet I had a feeling that they must be quite beautiful, quite noble. You will laugh! Do you know, you, who remember with emotion our Sunday afternoons at the Colonne concerts, what urged me to plunge deep into some remote corner of this plain of which I saw and knew nothing? The first few bars of "The Damnation of Faust" which I could never listen to without being moved to the verge of tears by their slow, melancholic majesty . . . I couldn't sleep that night. Alone, I was on the upper deck wrapped in my overcoat facing . . . a coffin covered with a huge black veil bordered with a silver braid and two flower wreaths. This symphony of blacks and whites beneath the moon, and on this glistening mirror, all this nautical apparatus painted with brilliant whites, the gaping jaws of the ventilators, the black banks of the river, the somber coffin appearing as a giant muted smudge, the moving silhouette of the captain surveying his bridge up there, and the sole whisper of the two pilots on the poop deck, and suddenly, rudely, and deliberately punctuating the path, the somber clang of the bell on the top deck each time a small light shone out of the water—a night light from one of those little windmills asleep on the river of which I will speak to you again—but this coffin, disquieting as it is with its two dark wreaths, would reveal to me again and again this conspiracy of silence and the horizontality of outlines—all this flooded the heart with a great calmness, troubled but occasionally by an aroused shudder or by taking heed of welled-up tears.

I questioned the captain, and in between the yawns of those who slept indifferently on the red velvet benches, I explained my wishes, saying I was a painter and was looking for a country that had retained its integral character.

His information was sufficiently promising for us to disembark on a floating raft at daybreak, at approximately half an hour's distance from the small city of Baja. Alongside the road in half-buried pastures huge, gray Egyptian-like oxen were grazing. When we emerged into the town square, next to a church in a clearly Hungarian version of baroque, we were overrun by a throng of pitifully impoverished pilgrims carrying banners with crosses on them. These tattered, bare-headed men and women were chanting with great lassitude psalms for the repose of their souls, and, after soliciting a few rare alms, departed toward some sacred place. At once we were in the swarming marketplace, more overcrowded with peasants then with merchandise, because here we noticed immediately that it takes one or two women squatting all day behind a little basket of fruit or vegetables to sell twenty sous worth of goods.

In the same way, we would often meet along the roadside two or three women who attended to the grazing of a single cow and in the cities an occasional old hag who led a goat by a string and made it feed on the grass growing between the paving. But already, beyond the baskets of cherries, vegetables, and the butcher's stall, Auguste caught sight of a flash of enamel and cried out just like Columbus's lookout-man: "Pots!"

There they were, countless numbers of them, arranged on the pavement like apples in a cellar. It wasn't easy to communicate with the vendors; we made our debut as pantomimes: up to now we had always managed by speaking German. Thus gestures replaced words, and everything went so well that a half-hour later, having walked many blocks under an already torrid sun, we came to this attic, out of *A Thousand and One Nights* where Alibaba, by good fortune, mispronounced a few words in the language of Wilhelm II of Hohenzollern, the emperor and priest of good taste. With hands all swollen from working with clay, our man gesticulated slowly and indifferently above the dark and mute crowd of his vases which had stood still since winter in the half-darkness of this decrepit timber shed.

Our choice made, we climbed back down the ladder, and he introduced us to his grandmother, who shook hands with us for a long time. Afterward, we visited rooms which everywhere revealed the big city's bad taste in bric-a-brac which, according to Auguste's theory, will become a cornerstone, a psychological cornerstone! Finally, we went to the little old man's workshop, where he never works except in winter because in summer he is busy with farm work. Very simple, very rudimentary, this workshop, and nested at the edge of an exquisite courtyard overgrown with roses, where there rises obliquely, imposingly, a black curved pole that, sloping downward, allows water to be drawn from the well. The curbstone of the well, dear sculptor, isn't of chiseled stone but stuccoed in white, and there are real red and blue flowers that adorn it with the exuberance of their thrust. They are marvelous, these villages of the great plain, and you can imagine their grand style. The streets belong to the plain, entirely straight, very broad, and uniform, cut at right angles, punctuated throughout by little balls of dwarfish acacias. The sun crumbles into them. They are deserted; life there is furtive, transient, as it is in the immense plain for which they serve as outlets, vital centers. In a way these appear like the enormous wings of a theater since everywhere high walls close them off. Try to understand their impressive unity and generous architectural character; only one material, a strong yellow stucco; only one style; a uniform sky along with the remarkable acacias of such a strange green. The houses are lined up, a little too narrow but very deep, each with its own low gable, but without a projecting roof, sitting like a pediment on an interminable wall where the crowns of trees brim over and branches of climbing roses fill with enchantment the courtyards behind them. Imagine these courtyards to be like a room, a summer room. Since all the houses are equally spaced from the enclosure wall, their windows open only on one side, behind an arcade. Thus each house has its own courtyard, and the intimacy in them is as perfect as in the gardens of the Carthusian Monastery of Ema where, you may recall, we had a fit of spleen.[5] Beauty, joy, serenity gather here, and a wide semicircular portal, closed by a door lacquered in either red or green that opens onto a spacious exterior! The trellis assembled from latticework casts a green shadow, its white arcades bring comfort, and the three great whitewashed walls, which are repainted each spring, make a screen as decorative as the background of Persian ceramics. The women are most beautiful; the men clean-looking. They dress themselves with art: flashing silks, notched and multicolored leather, white short-sleeved shirts with black embroidery work; the nervous legs and small bare feet are of such a fine, brown skin; the women move with a swinging of hips which unfurls, like the skirt of a dancing girl, the thousand folds in the short dresses where the silk flowers ignite under a sun of golden fire. This costume delighted us; the people contrasted and harmonized with the enormous white walls and with the flowerbeds of courtyards which make here and there a strangely successful complement to the distinguished appearance of the streets. While I describe all this to you, I return to my comparison of a moment ago, as I remember a large panel from Isfahan, sketched at one time in the Louvre, which depicted small women dressed in blue accented with yellow, and yellow striped with blue, passing the time in a garden: the sky is white, animating the entire surface; a tree spreads its yellow leaves, the branches of its sky-blue trunk blossoming out with white flowers and green pomegranates. The flowers in a deep green meadow are black and white, and their leaves yellow and blue. An extraordinary joy gushes from that unique setting. You know how that panel excited me!

This is how it looked behind this high wall of the potter of Baja and his neighbors; a wall punctured by a large round door for carriages and by a very small one for people that opened directly onto the arcade. Alone in the street, dotted throughout by the little acacias in the shape of green balls, between the exuberance of trellises and climbing roses, are quietly posed face to face, from one end to the other, the yellow triangles of the low gables.

I say to you, Perrin, that we, we others from the center of civilization, are savages, and with this I take leave of you.

# VIENNA

To succor the poor, the rich enjoy themselves. How I admire them! It would be ridiculous if they, too, were bored, for then the poor would be denied the spectacle of their diversions, and thus not even a fragment of humanity would cheer up.

Jean Rictus has already soliloquized on this subject in the second stanza of his great ballad.[1]

So today is "Blumen Tag," flower day, overflowing with colors and luxurious displays. The streets leading to the Prater are filled with a grubby crowd. The aisles beneath the arches of the trees on the endless avenue that demarcates the park given to the city by the emperor are filled with mobs of poor, so utterly out of work that they find the means to come here to exacerbate their grudges, or simply to satisfy their need for gaping. O poor people of Vienna (whom I came to know four years ago), not at all nice, sordid, with expressionless faces! We elbow them for three hours without ever managing to like them, since Auguste and I do not like to take pity. May my friends at *La Sentinelle* forgive me these fleeting, superficial impressions![2]

In the nave of the grand avenue, there is an outpouring of carriages and luxurious cars. Everything is smothered in flowers, and under these ephemeral bouquets, other ephemeral bouquets—as a poet would say, other flowers—young girls, beautiful women, smiling, somewhat depraved, perhaps a little inflamed by their desires. Gentlemen in black play second fiddle in this orchestra of colors, serving inevitably as the subjects for intrigues that culminate in roses tossed and lilies proffered cynically.

These Viennese festivals, all perfumed and morbid and steeped in an atmosphere of selfishness and aristocratic depravity, are described by Mr. William Ritter in *Leurs Lys et Leurs Roses.*[3]

As for us, overwhelmed by the afternoon heat, we observe things only superficially; without getting caught up in stylish flirtations, we simply take notice of the elegant many-colored carriages, in pinks, blues, or yellows, in greens or shocking reds, in black and white, gray and white, gray or white, or all white. In this explosion of colors are two very artful ladies being promenaded under a canopy of white poppies with black seeds.

We note that the natural flowers are eclipsed by the paper ones, which are very well made but out of scale. At a distance, in the sparkle of all these comings and goings, they appear like great tropical strangers surrounded by our European roses, irises, and the poisonous scent of our great lilies.

It is also clear that the purpose of these frivolous processions, in which insane sums of money are lavished on vain efforts of beauty, escapes us. For although a piquant detail may show itself, as a whole it lacks unity. This is understandable since nobody has given any thought to it. But the unity of the place[4] is so powerful that it saves the situation: from then on, it is a stunning procession that passes between the black colonnade of tree trunks bearing an immense barrel vault that recedes as far as the eye can see. The eye becomes confused, a little perturbed by this kaleidoscopic cinema where dance the most dizzying combinations of colors. It is, quite simply, chic Vienna enjoying herself, while poor Vienna watches the show . . .

Sunset, in the suburb full of trees; a very large courtyard stretches out, bordered by low pavillions which are punctuated by arcades. Two pylons mark the entrance and, making a facade, a yellow bar encloses it, punctuated by the orderly alignment of the dark green shutters. A great palace sits there, laid out according to the majestic taste of Louis XIV.[5]

We cross this great undisturbed area at the very heart of the palace and all of a sudden, without warning, the spectacle of a French garden unfolds, a breathtaking garden. Simple, almost threadbare, and yet colossal! A flowerbed that looks square, immensely wide, deep, very flat, and above it, we perceive in the shortened perspective the geometrical compartments and the embroidery of box hedges. Not a single tree disturbs this surface where all is spread out. Meanwhile left and right, two formidable walls of greenery suddenly rise up, trimmed to an uncompromising smoothness, uncompromisingly horizontal. They appear enormously high—disconcertingly so, when we watch at their base the colorful crowd strolling about. In the distance the eye is arrested by a hillock crowned by a pitiful colonnade. But, if one turns around, once again one faces the big yellow bar of its facade, the high, stately wall with its tranquil attic nobly erect and punctuated by the somber green of a multitude of closed shutters.

Filled with gloom, within this distinguished setting, the old aristocratic Vienna survives. In the somber and quiet halls where the furniture is covered by dust covers, the portraits on the walls whisper the pompous Schönbrunn memories of long ago—when in the courtyard the carriage horses pawed the ground and when between the compartments courtiers in their French embroidery busied themselves with their minute affairs like so many silk moths . . .

. . . A little amateur art lover shakes our hands. We have rung his doorbell with no reason but to satisfy our passion for impressionist paintings. Some of the little man's paintings are beautiful, and we tell him so profusely. The little collector who has squeezed such fabulous, hundred-thousand-franc paintings into minuscule frames must meet with cold disappointments! There are so many of these little daubs the size of a grandmother's Bible that he has snatched up here and there, sometimes for ten thousand crowns, sometimes for only five thousand. The people whom he guides along these celebrity-covered walls are delighted at the wrong times, and never give the proper praise. The lighting is terrible, the environment foul, and the furniture in bad taste. But the little collector has Manets, Courbets, and Delacroix! These gems of his fill him with an anxious pride which demands the acquiescence, admiration, and confidence of others, and he greedily swallows up our remarks.

Thinking about this little man, this environment, and these works of the masters, an uneasy feeling seizes us. Could it be that he was only a snob, a pathological collector, without any sound or thoughtful love of art?

Here we are in the street discussing collectors of paintings. Auguste must submit to the account of a similar visit that I made recently to Hagen in Westphalia, to a famous Maecenas who had the soul of a precursor.[6] In his villa, built by the great artist Van de Velde, live the works of modern titans.[7] In the great hall one awaits the master of the house in the touching company of five women offering mystical flowers to an enraptured child; on the threshold of this dwelling, Hodler's *The Chosen One* gives an inkling of the soul of the one who lives here;[a] in the music room there is a large Vuillard, tormented Van Goghs, and tranquil Gauguins; once again the walls, with the furnishings, set the mood.[8] Through the large window of the studio the bulging forms of a Maillol turn white under the garden light.

a. We are in 1910. (Editor's note: The correct date is 1911, but Jeanneret often mistakenly refers to this journey as being from 1910. This as well as other notes by Jeanneret, identified by raised lowercase letters in the text, date from July 1965, unless otherwise identified.)

There is not a single corner in this dwelling that does not enclose a dream. The impression is profound; little by little one is filled with admiration and with brotherly affection for this young man who smiles in this setting as he endeavors to suffuse everything with his superior intelligence and his goodness.

But let us take a look at contemporary Viennese painting. Let us cross over this threshold of an epoch, the "Secession." In the grand hall we encounter Monsieur Roll—of Paris![9] Monsieur Roll of Paris, one of the great national figures, that is, of the French, and guest of the Viennese Secession! Strange symbol for such a den! Our enthusiasm tucks in its wings and frantically searches along other exhibit walls for the manna of consolation. A useless effort—banality is rampant, mediocrity triumphant. Therefore, quick, let us pass again under the dome that once symbolized the triumphs of Klimt and Hodler, and once more on the Karlsplatz, contrite at having tossed twenty sous to the wind, we take off for the Hagenbund!

The Hagenbund, on another and less unpleasant note, shows us the efforts of another association of artists but teaches us nothing. Without hesitation we give up by common accord. Auguste is very angry, and I am very sad. The Künstlerhaus exhibits the Viennese reactionaries. My God, where can substance be found to stir the emotions? We proceed very tired to the work of Koloman Moser exhibited at Mietke's . . .

Ah, this modern Viennese painting, what a plague! We are really at a loss this time. Neither Luna Park nor Klein Venedig in the Prater will save us from this disaster! The Gallery of Modern Art, where some famous Frenchmen are exhibited, is closed!

It must be an inspiration from heaven that guides us along the pompously repugnant halls and corridors of the Imperial Gallery, and toward the great ribaldry of that powerful painter, the passionate lover of life, this man with his fantastic imagination, that grandiose stylist, and that astonishing impressionist, born three hundred years before Courbet, old Pieter Breughel himself, who sings from his innermost soul in his "Seasons" and his "Kermises," his joy of life, his love for this good Earth on which he likes to finds himself, and which gives him strength and delight because it is filled with beauty and health.

This is what we shall remember of Vienna's paintings, more than the splendid superficialities of Velasquez, more than the fleshiness of Rubens, so powerful in Munich, but repulsive here.

Vienna is noted for her music (I took ample advantage of it in the past, when Mahler was conducting at the opera house), and for her baroque architecture.[10] All those noble churches, those princely houses of the seventeenth and eighteenth centuries, are now disappearing. Invaded by modern buildings the environment is being butchered pitilessly, and one must seek refuge in the retreats of old French-style gardens of the Belvedere. Absentmindedly, I forgot the Augarten. Amid the bad taste that floods the boulevards with a bombastic, nouveau riche architecture, quintessentially Viennese, one can console oneself by seeking the latest creations of architects of the new school: works full of good sense but at the same time tremendously audacious. Again this solace is not accessible to everyone, because in the insane swarming of this too-dense city, one must possess an almost professional flair to discover these works.

So in the final analysis our impression of Vienna remains a dismal one. And despite our sincere effort to adjust, Vienna remains tarnished by an atmosphere of tasteless financial grandeur that burdens, crushes, and shocks. The Vienna of today remains dismal for us who have only passed through without penetrating its soul.

*Der Goldene Pelikan,*
*Jeanneret's hotel in Vienna*
*(courtesy FLC)*

# THE DANUBE

The Orient Express loses no time. It traverses one country, then another, bellowing and whistling for just a few minutes during its sad stopovers in the great railroad stations, and then continues on, insensitive to the natural beauties that jostle it, or that it disturbs. On both the trip out and the return, one must simply give up hope of ever seeing that Gloria Deo of the three incomparable mosques rising on the hill of Adrianople in that plain where the Maritsa flows. We give up on the Orient Express.

As on the map, a colossal river flows from the Alps to the Black Sea, rolling for days across plains which, we are told, are mostly deserted, and which it continually floods.

As on the map the red lines indicating the railroad tracks do not approach the winding blue meanders except here and there where they cross. To ensure the transit of rides and merchandise along the Danube's course, great white paddleboats have been built. They work up and down the river daily during the summer but less frequently in winter. The accommodations on board are very comfortable. The forward section, consisting of a hold where sleeping quarters and a restaurant are combined, comprises the second-class section. It also includes a smoking lounge and an open deck swept by strong winds. This section is separated from first class by the engine room, whose fetid emissions of burned oil envelop the peasants, crowded together with their unimaginable bundles; these are rugged and simpleminded men, dressed in ancestral fashion, who are now tasting the first fruits of a European civilization adorned, to their eyes, by all the fascinating allurements that will eventually disrupt their lives. We see their getups change at every border crossing—Austria, Hungary, Serbia, Bulgaria, Rumania. They vary from the wildly colorful embroideries of the *puszta* (the Hungarian plain) to the thick, dark fabrics of Serbia, from white furs to black ones, from white wools adorned with black to those that have kept the natural brown of the thousands of Balkan flocks from which they come. At times we see wild men covered with patches held to their bodies with a network of strings. To undress every day would be extremely awkward; it is these men who lie down with the sheep and horses beneath the stars on the gray *puszta* or in the arid Balkan.

First class on these big boats is quite good. Everywhere there is red velvet, tasteful decor. And there are flowers on the tables in the smoking lounge. And on the very wide deck, clusters of comfortable benches and rocking chairs can be found under a protective awning. One can eat and drink at modest cost. The price of the trip is negligible; we pay ten francs for a second-class student ticket from Vienna to Belgrade. Although we are no wealthier than Spanish tramps, we still have difficulty accepting the discomforts of the bow. Every time we climb aboard a boat, we tell the same simple story to the ranking officer in charge:

—Excuse us, Captain, but first class is outrageously finer than second; we feel that as students . . .

And they feel the same way, these high-ranking gentlemen, whether they be Viennese, Magyar, or Rumanian. It is thus that we travel down the Danube for only a few francs, in a rocking chair under a protective awning, seated on the velvets of the smoking lounge!

We embark at 10 p.m. from some corner of the Viennese suburbs with a crowd of peasants loaded with sacks and baskets, who, like us, would like to take advantage of this free night offered by the company, for the departure will not be until morning. These people have third-class tickets; they will pile up against each other, beside, above, and below their bundles, to keep warm on this deck prone to every wind.

This first night we do not enjoy the velvets already mentioned. The benches, where we quickly stretch out, are covered with oilcloth. Other travelers arrive who would like to jostle us aside, but we are sleeping deeply. Practically all night they work their revenge by playing cards, pounding their fists on the table, and using all those interjections that are customary in this kind of game. The cigars will create a dense haze as unbearable to the eyes as are the lights that are left burning. Then there will be an old man with a cold who shall cough endlessly and who, swearing, will persistently chase every five minutes after an imaginary vermin.

He is one of those people with preconceived ideas; on themes like this one, Europe generates certain legends about the East. And then, one expects everything to be filthy in these countries where things are, in fact, quite clean. Sometimes even Auguste raves at night while waging war against those invisible little beasts.

The more respectable travelers come aboard at dawn, and the boat sets out toward Budapest against a violent wind. What can I say about the trip. I who don't know how to write? The most I can say is that, being not yet very sensitive, I received broad but imprecise impressions, like those transmitted to us in their childish forms by terra-cotta made thousands of years ago by the early inhabitants of the lands from which I am writing. One must thoroughly master one's subject before attempting to evoke such impressions. Instead, I was enthralled and crushed. The impressions were, I must confess, considerable, and unexpected. Slowly they took hold of me. This journey toward Bucharest, which might have lasted only three days, took us two weeks. We remained on the deck constantly watching the unchanging spectacle, which slowly became more varied; our books remained closed on our laps. What a great happiness it was, what a serene joy. I must be forgiven these few lines, frail and inadequate as they are. The dirty tide of the big city was soon to become pearly white, then blue. We waltz delightedly to Strauss's "Blue Danube." What I had thought to be a sort of indigo blue was in fact a liquid pearl which turned opal in the evening. We came down the river on the rapid flow of this great tide. I imagined I was sailing up this river beyond the Alps, and remembered an evening when, leaving for Berlin—rather anxiously—I experienced a tormenting vision: from a cemetery that beamed at me, perched upon the mount of Donaustauf not far from the Ratisbon, the absolute immobility of a great red serpent clinging to the flat dark plain overrun by the night. So much calm pained me. Again in my imagination I was going down the river in the direction pointed by the bows. Belgrade lay at its elbow, the magic door to the East. Then came the tragic echoes of the march from Kazan, bleeding from worldly combat. The Iron Gates where the cohorts of Trajan raised their eagle banners.[1] I saw this inviolable gorge swoon in the golden Rumanian wheat, where even the sky is obliterated in the light and where all noise has been forever silenced. A little farther downstream, these floods bestowed themselves completely upon the East. Confused, I followed these vicissitudes which were to be my own.

The solitude is incredible. For hours at a time there is nothing to be seen to the left or the right but a line of trees along the horizon, tiny in the distance and blue in the light. The waves reach and submerge them. Fjords appear to open out, bringing sky into this tiny land. Like a white ghost, our boat floats in an elusive element. How can one differentiate this sky from the water that absorbs it? All animation is only in the sky: a drama of clouds which is repeated by the water and droned through the veil of waves.

Not a house, not a boat sailing upstream. Sometimes, however, an impressive tugboat appears together with its barges on their dark and solemn march; from time to time we come upon a small pontoon serving as a cabin for the watchman. A road scurries away toward the great *puszta*. Carriages wait at the landing pier with fiery warhorses and coachmen, proud and bedizened Hungarians who once had belonged to Attila's hordes. They remove their harnesses; they leave with their horses and go off in a whirlwind of dust. Silence is restored.

Solitude again. Right in the middle of the river is a row of mills built on moored boats—charming little mills sitting tightly together like an ark; they are flanked by a large wheel, wider than it is high and built of lightweight hoops equipped with gray paddles, as gray as the ark beside the luminous gray of the landscape. They recall China, these little mills, as fine and delicate as basketwork.[2]

In the morning an epic, sphinxlike rock appeared. Upon its tremendous crest a long column supported a Virgin, while its back of closely cropped turf bristled with rough, brown, perforated sod, the remains of antique walls and awful dungeons. Pressburg had raised upon a mountain the cube of its fortress.[3] Later, this warlike apparition collapsed into the blue and the gray of the plain. Again the *puszta,* stretched out, endlessly.

It is like being on the Amazon, so remote are the river banks and so impenetrable are their forests. The little round clouds of the afternoon open whitish eyes. There is now nothing to see but a horizontal line; the river's bends make it continuous from one side to the other! Were I a fisherman or merchant along its banks, I would religiously sculpt out of wood, somewhat in a Chinese manner, a god who would be this river and whom I would worship. I would set him on the bow of

*Tomb of Emma L'Eplatte-nier, aunt of Charles L'Eplattenier, in the Rere-pesi Cemetery outside Budapest (courtesy Bibliothèque de La Chaux-de-Fonds)*

*The Cathedral of Eszter-*
*gom, "a cube and a dome*
*supported by many col-*
*umns " (courtesy FLC)*

my boat, smiling and gazing out vaguely ahead of him, just as they did in Norman times. My religion, however, would not be one of terror: it would be serene but above all full of admiration.

Estergom appeared, strangely silhouetted; a cube and a dome supported by many columns.[4] From afar, each of them hints at some marvel. A cube animated by a wonderful rhythm, and which the rising mountains present, like an offering on this altar that they themselves make for it.

Finally, under a green sky, at the hour when everything surrenders to poetry, there appeared in the river an immense fan of black and gold blades within the diluted pink of great tides; and, looming, mountains with willful profiles were surrounding us, purple evocation of a Greece we had envisioned as similar but more architectural. Because, over there, the mountains will be of stone and the fan shall be the sea.

We got off in Vác, nestling so gently in the foliage of acacias.[5] It would not be fitting to end this unforgettable day in Budapest. By noon of the following day, we are suffocating in the heat of the plain. A suburban train brings us slowly toward Budapest. It is full of peasants in their Sunday finery. Handsome men, young and excitable, are dressed in shiny black close-fitting garments. They wear three or four roses in their lapels or on their hats. The women are dark-skinned and energetic, as if made out of some tough substance. Their costume is low keyed. They also hold in their hands roses of flesh-color, blood, amber, or alabaster. Decorative panels are painted against the black of their aprons, similar to those found in the art of rich peasants of the eighteenth century, which one sees in the historical museums.

Why should I speak of Budapest, since I neither understood nor liked her? She appeared to me like a leprous sore on the body of a goddess. One must climb to the citadel to see the irreparable condition of this aborted city. One is surrounded by a vibrant organism of palpitating mountains. A generous outpouring of nacreous fluid rises up slowly from the plain. The Danube encircles the mountains, condensing them into a powerful body that faces the boundless expanses of the plain. But over this plain there spreads a dull black smoke into which the network of streets disappears. Eight hundred thousand inhabitants have rushed here in the last fifty years. And disorder in pompously deceitful forms has rendered this city suspect. Some people admire the immensity of its public buildings. I can't, shocked as I am from the outset by their display of such differing and discordant styles. They line the river banks but they are not sufficiently in concert to offer her a harmonious procession. On the heights of the city a monstrous palace leans against an ancient church recently restored.[6]

However, on this same mountain, closer to this citadel, ancient huts appear like a blossoming among the acacias. These simple dwellings are united by walls behind which trees shoot up. These dwellings spring up naturally on this undulating ground. We spend hours on this peaceful hill watching Taban, invaded by the night, light up with the quiet little lights of evening gatherings. There was a great calm. Suddenly there arose a slow and inexpressibly sad chant. It was a saxophone or an English horn; I listened with an emotion greater than one feels when the shepherd plays on his flute his old song at Tristan's death. What a strange and grandiose melody in the still landscape![7]

Do you know, readers, that my beautiful Danube was mutilated by an editor and a pair of scissors? Little gray mills had greatly impressed me the night of our voyage from Budapest down to Baja. In the moonlight there was a grand conspiracy of silence, of black and white, and of immutability. The lookout had punctuated the silence with the sound of a tragically lonely bell each time the distant light of a hanging lantern appeared suspended above the waves.

Of all that, the editor's scissors at *La Feuille d'Avis* of La Chaux-de-Fonds permitted you to see only a simpleton wrapped up in an overcoat like Napoleon, standing in the moonlight braced against the north wind, alone facing a coffin! And with all that, he forgot to write in the "To be or not to be," which might have been declaimed in such circumstances.[8] And then—to finish with this typographer!—the courtyards in Baja offered you the unpleasant sensation of an incoherent, incomprehensible description! Poor courtyards! Remove a man's head, part of his torso, and a leg, then paint a portrait of him. The streets of Baja, great channels open to the plain, were turned into "diversions" of this plain instead of "overflows." I recognize that the scissors were acting benevolently, aiming only to purify an uncertain style. I acknowledge their charitable intentions but decline their offer of help. For— allow me just one further word, weary reader—I do not offer you literature, since I have never learned to write. Having educated my eyes to the spectacle of things, I am trying to tell you of the beauty I encountered with sincere words. And my style is muddled just as my comprehension of things which is, itself, still muddled. The first day, this typographer wanted to avoid the wrath of an uncle! Because one of my uncles would take offense if I should confess to you our differences of opinion. In this first article therefore the typographer wanted a *friend* to be persuaded of the distortions in my thinking, rather than an *uncle*. But it was an uncle, and that makes it all the more amusing. If we had to spend our whole life without ever squabbling a little with our own kin, their vengeance would surely make itself felt at the reading of their will, owing to so much indifference!

Lastly, I would also like you to read in the paragraphs devoted to traditional pottery, that its color is *often*—but not *always*—symbolic. Here I go again, talking about pottery! This is a fatal tendency that leads me away from my path! In watching out for Charybdis, I run into Scylla!—and so we will continue our voyage down the Danube between Baja and Belgrade: the waves bite into prairies stretching far into the distance, perforated by pools of water and strewn with enormous gray spheres; giant water willows adhered to trunks of such a diameter and so gnarled that one would think they were rocks. Horses populate these vast expanses which are covered by flocks of geese as if by snow. All things meet again within a horizontal line, over which they accumulate and into which they merge. It's like, in geometry, a plane seen through a horizontal section. This plane is the endless *puszta* teeming with life. A few herons rise heavily and unfold, resembling the decorative scenes chiseled with so much exactitude in Japanese woodcuts. Rarely, not too high, an eagle passes by.

At one point we become quite excited over an aesthetic issue: a student of architecture from Prague, whom we met the day before, rails against certain iron bridges thrown boldly across the water. It's always the same type of bridge: a long rigid girder, perforated throughout, a masterpiece of lightness and engineering.[a] And because he imagines the atmosphere of the office in which these girders and bolts were calculated, our man has nothing but scorn for them. We defend the beauties of modern engineering and tell him about all the new possibilities of plastic expression and the bold realizations owed to it by the arts, and the splendid vistas it offers to the builder henceforth

a. One of these bridges is the work of Eiffel.

liberated from classical servitude. The Gallerie des Machines in Paris, the Gare du Nord, and the station in Hamburg as well, automobiles, aircraft, ocean liners, and locomotives seem conclusive arguments to us. But the man remains angry; he misses the acanthus leaf and the cast-iron Poseidon upon these long girders which flow as smoothly as an express train and which neither restrain the spirit nor disturb it longer than necessary.

They announced Belgrade during the night. And for two entire days we rid ourselves of our illusions about it, but how surely, how definitively: for it is a city a hundred times more undefined than Budapest! We had imagined a door to the East, swarming with colorful life, populated by flashing and bedizened horsemen wearing plumes and lacquered boots!

It is a ridiculous capital, worse even: a dishonest city, dirty and disorganized.[b] Its position is admirable, however, like that of Budapest. In a quiet corner of the city there is an exquisite ethnographic museum, with carpets, clothing, and . . . pots, beautiful Serbian pots of the kind we will go looking for in the highlands of the Balkans around Knjaževac. One gets there by a little Belgian railway, hanging precariously and vertiginously along the Bulgarian frontier. Alongside this track, in its own ravine, they are building a new so-called strategic line. It is directly within the range of the Bulgarian guns and will undoubtedly force the closing of the Belgian line within a year. The French engineer who tells

b. This impression is from 1910; I was 23. Serbia had been enslaved by the Hapsburgs for a long time. The revolt exploded in Sarajevo (June 1914) and triggered World War I, 1914–1918. (Editor's note: The real date is 1911, not 1910, and the note itself dates from 1965. Jeanneret is apologizing for his negative impressions of Belgrade back when he first saw it.)

*The Serbian countryside*
*(courtesy FLC)*

us all this, while drilling a tunnel, would like to weep in the face of such an absurdity.

We continue on foot and by cart. This Serbian countryside is ideal! The roadways are fragrant with camomile. The wheat rustles the plain, and then on the high plateaus endless fields of corn form an expansive, indolent, and weary arabesque on the purplish-black of the farmland. The cemetery at Negotin is quintessential. We must talk about cemeteries, but let us wait until Stamboul.

The gorge of Kasan is a joke, a bit of bluffing made by resounding words. A friend wrote me this winter in Berlin, "and even a stormy black sky and thunderbolts were unable to improve upon it."

O Gates of Iron! We didn't find you, or rather we didn't know how to make you come to life again. A modern and quite botched-up dam will be seen as your flagrant stigma of a soulless technician's philistinism, and you are forever denied the privilege of being evocative. Trajan scratched your rocks a little and carved—yes—a very beautiful inscription.

And the Danube was quite different as it flowed out from there: violent, dark, turbulent. This is Bulgaria. Facing it, there are also dunes, naked and agitated: this is Rumania. Silence and solitude cling stubbornly to this tragic soul uplifted by a swell. Before the river's bend at Belgrade, it was so serene, so blue! Here there are only rounded and sometimes collapsed ridges of yellow earth, which in places the grass attempts to cover. Not a tree, not a shrub anywhere: only aridity in all its imposing grandeur. No houses. The only sign of life this morning is the turbulent motion of the river which, bristling with foamy crests, is beating against austere and mute banks. A hillock suddenly moves and collapses. We think it is some sudden avalanche or the collapse of dark sand: it is a large flock of sheep that a shepherd—only a black speck against the sky—is pushing ahead of him.

A village is nestled in a kind of oasis, lying in a valley between two or three dunes. Purplish blue roofs and freshly painted facades disappear beneath the acacias. We are now two weeks out of Vienna; in the evening we shall be in Bucharest. We shall no longer see the great river, our new friend. In a week we shall cross it for a few minutes to go into Bulgaria, and aiming at the Shipka Pass, we shall resolutely descend toward the East.

We have stopped at Negotin, in Serbia, in the courtyard of an inn, enclosed by white walls and covered with a trellis. The shade is green upon the tablecloths. Outside the noon sun is grilling the plain. About thirty guests, all burghers of this lost little town, are celebrating a wedding and observing a bored tranquility. Every now and then, some speechifiers attempt a toast that lacks zest. Nevertheless a fat and ruddy man delivers a virulent harangue while rolling his eyes furiously until approval is expressed by various appropriate noises. But some tziganes are there, ten or fifteen men grouped at the head of the table. They play and sing strange music almost without stopping. It is with difficulty that our ears accustom themselves to these assonances and these new rhythms; western musical education limits itself too much to our own creations, and what's more, concerts offer only a few of them, an average of what is considered good taste, with nothing too new and also nothing of the music of former times.

Meanwhile, the courtyard is filled with sounds, and in a few quarters of an hour there I am, entirely captivated and enthusiastic. My recollections of the Russian chapel are awakened. There, they had new arrangements, infinitely more decorative, as powerful and high-pitched sopranos, women's choirs, head voices, and little children's choruses.

The timbre of this music is also new to us, not because of their instruments, which are similar to ours, but rather because of their rhythmic and harmonic arrangements. Then, too, this is a musical symbolism of which we know nothing and which we would find impossible in our era of individualism. Just as through Slavianski Agrenev we had heard immense, slow rivers rolling over the endless steppes, so at Negotin I hear the voice of the god that I would have worshipped on my boat: the Danube and the *Puszta* that embraces it—he, the serene ruler. Or rather, these are hymns to this god; they are the sighs, languors, and violent emotions of his people, camped on these vast lands which enforce mobility, endless vagrancy, and a freedom that is envious, extreme, and complete and that awakens a feeling of great dignity in every soul. A nation sings, crouching near the ashes of a hearth in pink, green, and blue twilights, and surrenders to the burning soul that moves it. This plain, these steppes, and these flowers, which awaken only the feeling of things without permitting their perception, could only be expressed by music, the art of subjectivity and dreams. Our beautiful Danube is deified in the song and the play of the tziganes. The form is that of a Hungarian czardas—violins, cellos, and double basses, but no diabolical cymbals. Standing, the conductor, a folksinger, sings the song of his people. He forms groups according to the emotion that stirs him; its elements are centuries-old. Nothing is determined in advance. He presents his credo, and the others wail, swoon, or cry out, faithful to his thought. The same thrill vibrates through this handful of sensualists.

The solo voice relates a gentle thought—or perhaps it is a solitary "mi" note. Suddenly the group takes off, and a cube of music comes out of it; all the voices start in unison, and the instruments ornament the background with pizzicati or serpentine arabesques.

The singer recites a new thought that moves the czardas, and they all dissolve into tears over these somber chords.

Alone, the singer sings a dream of hope; and joy surges up like an awesome tower surrounded by flaming steel and clashing arms under the glorious sun.

But then the great river overflows: the solemn voice sends quivers to the fat strings of the double bass, and while a solo voice rises like an elegy, night falls, all blue; the infrangible horizon separates while bringing together, far away, the humming earth and the sky illuminated with stars.

Only the singer is still standing. Everything has ended in an awesome geometry. Bach and Handel reached the same heights and so did the Italians of the eighteenth century. The hymns were like huge squares laid down or like towers. And crenelated walls with running arabesques connected them. In fact yesterday morning we saw at the river's edge twenty-six squared towers flanking a massive forbidding wall.

The ruby-red wine from the bottles we empty in the inn's courtyard is exquisite, originating from Bordelais wine stocks tended on the hillside by French specialists. They too are artists, these winegrowers who make it possible for men to pour into their stomachs all of these little shares of paradise, which, as a matter of fact, cause us to wander and wobble a little. Anyway, it is only animals who always walk in a straight line and never take leave of their senses! They do not play the music of the Moulin Rouge for these two people getting married. Bravo! But it seems to me that the people surrounding them (parents, friends), bothersome or indiscreet, sense their uselessness in this place. They drink a lot of this ruby-red wine to overcome their uneasiness; they want either to feel happy on a day designated as festive or simply to sink into a reassuring torpor. I also drank my part of the good little wine of Negotin, and lost in a reverie, I sense a psychic drama uniting these six beings—a man, a woman, two mothers, two fathers—in this courtyard where the tziganes allow the race, the great nation of the dead, to speak through their age-old songs. The tziganes sing out to the newlyweds in voices heavy with sentiment; and their music separates them from these fools who have been assembled here by a ridiculous custom. I would like to see them go to the devil, these nuisances! I would like to see these two mothers, from whom a son and a daughter are being taken, and these two fathers who, just as in the time of the patriarchs, conclude an alliance and unite their stock, and these newlyweds, who are about to receive the ultimate gift, I would like to see them not speaking, eating but a little light food, avoiding the traps laid by cunning wines, seated in a white room with bare walls. At that, the chant of the vast plain would rise up to proclaim the immutability of all things, and the voice of the river would tell of eternal life. The great stanzas would fill the bare white room, and the sap of their people would pervade the sensibilities of their hearts. When the pattern of the melodic lines resolves itself, I would like to see the two mothers go away mingling tears of joy with tears of regret and the two fathers citing the past and speaking of the future. As for these two beings, who in the course of days past and days to come will not have any other moment comparable to this one, I would like them to remain alone together in this bare white room.

Auguste continued to extract the ruby-red wine from the little vials. But, oddly enough, he couldn't take it and he was sick that evening!

# BUCHAREST

(Letter to a lady who told me one day of her admiration for Carmen Sylva, Queen of Rumania.)

Madam,

I remember neither where nor when it was! But surely Carmen Sylva had just published some exquisite book, as *Les Annales* put out the portrait of the poet-queen. You then had been moved by the simplicity of her finery and the delicacy of her gray hair and her gracious, hospitable eyes. *Les Annales* had loudly proclaimed what an artist's soul was burning behind that modest appearance.

Well, here I am about to destroy your idol, Madam, for I have seen the palace in which she shines! You will agree, won't you, that the walls of a dwelling reflect the soul that inhabits it, and taking into account that I only judge by what my eyes show me, having read me you will forgive me!

After all, you know El Greco! Precisely: Domenikos Theotocapoulos. He has been revived for three or four years now. The miracle took place at the Salon d'Automne of 1908.[1] This retrospective and rehabilitative exhibition was really a great joy for art lovers. For art historians focused on the works of painters like Murillo, Zurbaran, and Velasquez, El Greco was a scarcely noticed chronological incident. The above-mentioned valets had impudently raised their heads before the master for three hundred years! And yet Cézanne is already dead! He was one of those who liked El Greco the most and drew out of him the modernism that had been inscribed on his canvases for three hundred years. As a matter of fact the great salons of painting of the second half of the nineteenth century every year resolutely closed their doors to the genius of Cézanne. This honorable man had to die as the laughingstock of the crowd—also, it is true, as the high priest of the sanctuary whose congregation has descended from Courbet and Manet.

My God! Even on that occasion the Paris crowd acted no differently from any other! It was expressing as it so often does this solid common sense which sanctifies mediocrity and instinctively revolts against any original efforts. How happy this Paris crowd would be to banish these poets, these painters and sculptors, these musicians who rekindle the great hearthbed of art in the midst of ingratitude. Roman Rolland wrote an entire book to reveal to Paris its strength and to bring this home to the crowd. Meanwhile on the threshold—on the fashionable boulevard—the crowd carries its heroes shoulder high, and then goes off to the two official salons to satisfy itself with pictorial literature. Each year, ten thousand fresh canvases, where the muses of banalities are free to flutter, arouse the crowd's curiosity. For a good laugh, this crowd goes on to the Salon d'Automne, and to the Salon d'Indépendants—once epic battlefields.[2] They think they are at the circus and they laugh . . . because they see what they believe to be the unbearable stupidity of those admired by their own sons!

Having said all that with brash immodesty, you will understand, Madam, how much I believed in the excellence of Carmen Sylva, since by crossing the threshold of her residence, I was going to find eight paintings by El Greco hung from the walls of her private rooms and her music room.

I will not tire you with a description of these paintings, but I will try to stay with the subject to describe to you their settings, settings whose colors could have been born from Cézanne, with those animated groupings, strange lines, disconcerting forms and blotches—transcending the Spanish aristocratic attitude filtered through Hellenic blood and a grandiose sensuality of Catholic mysticism in feverish flesh. The time period is that of Philip the Catholic, and the settings are Toledo and the Escorial.[3] One cannot imagine El Greco without this age and this architecture. Time has passed, but Toledo remains, with its red moraine whose stones are houses cascading down the sides of a rock standing on a red plateau bordered by blue-black or ash-gray mountains. A deep gorge at the foot of the walls makes an unlit furrow. A heavy sky lays its ultramarine sheet over this desolate land. It is rugged like a terra-cotta split by too much heat. But beneath this tough crust the walls offering the El Grecos refuge in the icy mystery of the white chapels are uniform and whitewashed. White, raw, impassive, they are the necessary and majestic environment for such glowing painting.

As we ascended the grand staircase in the palace of Carmen Sylva, we could hardly believe it was real. It was so ugly. We went past God knows how many rooms in whose jumble we found the El Grecos we were seeking.

Of the eight we were supposed to see, four, unfortunately, were at Sinaia, the summer residence. The rooms we passed through were cramped and messy. Countless curios, from floor to ceiling, were accumulated, all the paraphernalia of "Homaisian" raptures.[4] We couldn't believe our eyes. Here and there, always in some dark and out-of-the-way corner, the servants would point out a Saint George or a Nativity or a Marriage of the Virgin for which Auguste had undertaken this journey. Numerous crude paintings infamously occupied places of honor, and dispersed on the furniture could be seen photographic portraits, as in the apartment of my concierge in Paris. I took note, so you would believe me, Madam, of the room in which the *Marriage of the Virgin* is located. The dimensions are three meters wide and six deep. Half the room is elevated by the height of a step, and separated from the rest by means of a wooden colonnade hung with curtains. It is behind these curtains that you will find the painting, but not on the illuminated wall which was deemed more suitable for a painting of the same size showing an episode from the Franco-Prussian War replete with smoke, cannons, pointed helmets, and dead soldiers. The French in retreat! The two paintings are one meter apart. All along a shelf running around the room may be seen about sixty wooden soldiers in various outfits. Facing the El Greco is a rather large fireplace—of wood—made only for effect! In front of the El Greco, and hiding it a little, is a bust of the queen in white marble. On the tables are an almanac, some photographs clustered together, and some frames made of leather or plush. Wall ledges of barely sufficient width are loaded with pottery and that wretched glassware on which stupid-looking grotesque masks may be seen emerging out of Louis XV shells. Then right next to them there is some superb peasant pottery from Walachia. Now imagine the ceiling, supported by heavy false wooden corbels, and then count with us, in this three-by-six-meter space divided into two levels: seven tables, an enormous lectern, three cupboards, seven armchairs. We noticed these armchairs were covered with red plush, feet and back included. Fringes and tassels announce the affluence of the owner to one and all.

In the music room, to which young protegés drawn from Europe by the Maecenaen queen go to play as in a temple, it's worse, I swear. It's not to be believed! And as for the fourth El Greco that shines there—it's a fake!

That is why I no longer believe in *Les Annales,* Madam, or in Carmen Sylva. What is more, this lady is from an altogether too respectable German family and seems to be devoid of artistic taste. Her husband and her palace are totally out of place on the burning pavements of Bucharest which speak of so many things. Forcefully, they tell of the supremacy of the flesh, and a certain implacable sensuality is forced upon them. Bucharest is full of Paris; but there is so much more here. The women are beautiful to behold, beautifully coiffured even in the harsh light and all decked out in exquisite dresses. To us they are not like strangers whose costumes alone would create a barrier. During the long promenade along the via Victorii, upon their return from the races, they would recline gracefully in the carriages, in their Parisian dresses made of sumptuous but sober fabrics, their big hats, black, gray, or blue with enormous floppy feathers, or tiny toques placed over overgrown hair, and their eye makeup and lipstick always of a muted color, as aristocratic in appearance as the beautiful bodies beneath the caress of the fabrics—all these things urged us to notice and to admire them—and with the same sentiment we recalled seductive visions of fashionable Paris. One senses that, inevitably, everything here encourages the cult of the woman, and it seems that because of her beauty, she alone is the great goddess of this city.

Do not make fun of me, Madam, if I am still dazzled. What is more, the persistent fragrance of lilies lingers everywhere—the lilies sold by the tziganes. Here again are those splendid women! Yellowish complexions under black hair, eyes with which bewitching words are uttered. Light and simple garments from which emerge hands with coral-painted fingernails that contrast with the ivory of the lilies. For us, the tziganes will become a symbol, the only possible expression of this city in which we were so tortured.

Innumerable teams of carriage horses paw the ground. The coachmen—all eunuchs, very fat and speaking in high-pitched voices—drive their splendid, spirited horses through the crowded calei. All these coachmen are almost upright, draped in dark-blue velvet togas. The clatter of a thousand hooves on the hard pavement is a music or a rhythm which is almost as loud during the night.

What can I tell you about this tree-filled city that stretches extensively out but offers always the closed appearance of a middle-class neighborhood? The buildings are not more than three stories high, and the streets end quickly. The architecture is paltry, like life itself in these parts. The Beaux-Arts style is pervasive because only architects who have graduated from Paris work here. It may be trite, but it is not ugly. Because of its unity of conception, Bucharest isn't as heterogenous and ugly as German cities. One's eyes are arrested by neither the familiar contours nor the garlands that we all know by heart. These are entirely free and offer themselves to any celebrity who passes by. In Bucharest every day of the week is Sunday.

Using the free language of the Sunday painter, let me tell you in three lines, Madam, with colors and daubs about the soul of this city where stern hearts are tormenting themselves. On the terrace of a cafe we met the famous painters and writers of Rumania. Since we were French, we were received very graciously.[5] These painters were those of the "Rumanian Youth," also a "Secessionist group," which came all the way here. We liked them because they spoke to us fervently about their national arts, and we thrilled together on the subject of traditional embroideries and ceramics.

Then we went by ourselves to see, under the Rotunda, the challenge that these young artists were making with their revolutionary works to all those who are obsessed by routine. Well, those imbeciles!—they have allowed themselves to be assassinated by Europe! We had to put up with entire walls of Munich academism, and moldings loaded with dull paintings brought over from the quai Voltaire.[6] These young people who, before revolting, had the good fortune to be born on the shore of the Dobrudja and to frolic around in the *vias* and the *caleie,* they forgot—when they did wish to speak about their "inner selves," standing in front of a canvas holding the orgiastic palette—they forgot the cravings of their flesh and their thirst for Byzantine debaucheries. Their hearts were not flooded by the rude fragrance of the lilies sold by the beautiful tziganes! Their canvases are "trash" (allow me this rich word). Why didn't they just paint the trash around them, and in a plastic tzigane idiom, in awesome colors where lemon yellows drowned in dirty greens would have inflamed rotting purples? There, the white of the lilies and the crimson of the nails would have been like screams. The great and imperial black would have invaded and framed this swooning of colors. And in it, the incomparable pink would have come to spread itself—this pink that all primitive and healthy peoples adore and use lavishly because it is the color of real flesh. This painting, like the sickly smiles of the tziganes, would have been made rhythmic with simple figures. And seeing it, one would have known how hot it is here, and how strong the call of the city is—so strong that the arteries almost burst and the brain explodes, and one cannot sleep at night!

# TŬRNOVO[1]

Everywhere Bulgaria is like a garden. Along the railroad track is a wild border of hollyhocks, yellow buds, and azure hemp and chicory, red poppies, and scabiosa. The big thistles make a wine-colored layer in the white flower beds and among the tufts in bloom. The wheat comes right to the edge of the track. In the distance runs a line of evenly spaced fruit trees, yellow lakes swept by the hot west wind. But once the train reached the high plateaus, everything became harsh again.

At sunset I climbed the huge rock on which the town is built—a tumultuous moraine of houses crimped by paths. The wind was blowing, marking the bounds of the high plateau that the train crossed at a right angle to the Danube; mountains rose up suddenly, formed of foundations of narrow stones submerged in immense sand banks. A deep cleft, almost a canyon, crenelated by rocks in horizontal layers, lets the yellow river flow through. From these dry heights where only camomile blooms and sends out its fragrance, in the opening of the great portal whose rocky feet drop straight down, we see the plain. The sun has set right there, and all the way down it bleeds into a great horizontal line: it must be the Danube over there. On the other side, in a semicircle, the Balkans froth and swell at this hour so exquisitely blue. A frieze of light cobalt marks this highest mountain where the Shipka winds its way, the gateway to Turkey which we shall enter on horseback in a few days.[2] At the foot of this mountain where I am lying, the yellow ribbon of the river encloses the town, following the nervous path of a figure eight. Here the stream spreads out to form little islands of sand; there, drawn together again, rapids disturb it. Droves of huge oxen are immersed in the river. The oxen are gray, with almost white stomachs and black spines gently modulating into the color of their flanks. Their eyes have the softness and beauty of gazelles' eyes, and their horns crown them with a majesty in the

A peasant's dwelling in
Shipka, the gateway to
Turkey (courtesy FLC)

manner of Egyptian bas-reliefs. By noon, we had seen hundreds of black buffaloes lying in the muddy ooze of the river. They were sleeping, immersed in the muddy water, offering us an unexpected sight. Their heads always stretch out horizontally and their white eyes seem to be contemplating lugubrious thoughts under their dark fore- heads. For such a tremendous size, they have a startling color, somber as a funeral veil, opaque as tainted ink, and it is frightening to see them approaching with their horns turned back and their snouts full of froth. I understand why these tragic animals were harnessed to the Chariot of Death, the Chariot of Vanity, and the Chariot of Vice by the fifteenth-century painter of those famous panels in the Academy of Sienna which we looked at with fascination.[3] At that time we believed them to be the pure invention of an inspired painter.

At the bottom of the canyon, the herdsmen have entered the water to drive before them the oxen overcome by the heat. Through the huge rocky door, my eyes wander for the last time along this dark horizon which marks Europe, and I again climb down these slopes where a cascade of houses tumbles down.

What an extraordinary town of which no one has ever spoken, lost far from the major lines of communication! Auguste says it is as fine as Avila in Spain. It was the medieval residence of the czars of Bulgaria. Tŭrnovo is no village. It is made of thousands of houses; they are fastened onto the ridges of precipitous rocks and then piled up, rising one over the other all the way to the top of this towerlike mountain. The walls are white and their frames black, and the roofing is like the bark of a tree. Seen from afar it is an arid stratification, some larger white spots signal the churches, not Byzantine but Baroque, and related to the exquisite architecture of the Bavarian and Tyrolese mountains. We spent a long time wandering through the streets of Tŭrnovo, whose exceedingly picturesque character remains attractive because of their perfect cleanliness. There is nothing I detest so much as the village that attracts the "literalism" and the sentimentalism of so many painters just because dung invades the alleys and mud has splattered as high as the roofs. Such filth always betrays a base negligence, and one can be certain that the inhabitants who allow themselves to vegetate in such a place are poor and do not cultivate any art.[4] When the blood is young and the mind healthy, normal sensuality asserts itself. Men work less and search for well-being. They take care of their dwellings with a solicitude that, to us, would appear exaggerated. They want them to be clean, gay, and comfortable: they adorn them with flowers. They dress in embroidered clothing whose flamboyant colors tell of their joy of life. Their dishware is florid and artistic, and rugs, woven by the women following age-old tradition, cover floors that are scrupulously maintained. And each spring, the house that one loves receives its new coat: sparkling white, it smiles the whole summer through foliage and flowers that owe to it their dazzle.

At Tŭrnovo the rooms are whitewashed, and the white is so beautiful that I was very impressed. Already last year I had become enthused over the decorative power that people and things take on when seen against the white of peasant rooms. Serbia, Rumania, Bulgaria, Constantinople, and Athos, from which I have just returned, have once again confirmed this impression.[5] At Tŭrnovo they whitewash each room before Easter and Christmas, and in that way the house is always bright.

Each house has its main room; a very large window, wider than it is tall and checkered with windowpanes, opens out on the trees and flowers of the garden, and because of the unique location of this town,

*Houses in Tŭrnovo,*
*"fastened onto the ridges*
*of precipitous rocks"*
*(courtesy FLC)*

the bold and brutal profile of the mountain and a yellow stream are framed in the geometry of the fenestration. These rooms are so small that the window takes up the entire wall, and a balcony is always hung, overlooking the avalanche of houses; this balcony is of fine woodwork, and the contours of the pillars and of the glaze brings to mind the exquisite niches of Islamic interiors. In this charming small space, the men squat on sofas and quietly smoke. They look like a Persian painting in a Moorish setting. The garden door is pink and green; the enclosure is no larger than a room, and a trellis covers it all. There are roses and tulips, and then many lilies of a perfidious fragrance, carnations, and hyacinths. Slabs of white stone pave the ground wherever the flowers have not invaded. I have already said that the walls are white, and sometimes blue, like the deepest part of the sea.[a]

Toward evening we entered one of the small churches preceded by a light blue porch. On the iconostasis shone twenty-nine icons from their golden heavens and the halos of their saints, each set in a golden niche that a Hindu or a Chinese could have sculpted. They were of the most beautiful style, more Italian than Byzantine, and would serve as a good transition between Cimabue and Duccio.[6] One feels quite moved before such an ensemble, in the dim of a sanctuary at such a beneficent moment. I was as intoxicated here as I have so often been in the little gallery of the Italian primitives in the Louvre, where the Great Madonna is an object of faith and where, after having preached to the birds and the little animals of the forest, Saint Francis, thunderstruck with ecstasy, receives the stigmata.

a. I have since learned that custom requires whitewashing during the great religious holidays, a useful regulation! The blue framing around the doors and windows drives away the flies.

*Interior of a house in Tǔr-
novo (courtesy FLC)*

*A Baroque-style monastery in Gabrovo, Bulgaria, June 1911 (courtesy FLC). One of thirteen watercolors exhibited under the title "Langage de Pierre" in Munich (1911), Neuchâtel (1912), Zurich (1913), and Paris (at the Salon d' Automne, 1913)*

The next day we had a great delight: in a village at the foot of the blood-colored Shipka, we were able to buy from a poor priest a few old icons on which golden halos glitter against fiery skies. Afterward the Balkans disappointed us by being green and blue, leafy, and covered with forests, when we had wanted them to be red and pitiless, red like an earth that has drunk so much blood, as red as is necessary for an attack by bandits to have any pictorial quality. Alas! There weren't even any bandits! In the night, holding our horses by their bridles, we climbed down rough slopes, and we collapsed at the only inn around, where dreadfully filthy men were already asleep on every bench. And because strangers almost never wander onto these remote roads, they were very ill at ease when receiving us. To tell the truth, though, this uneasiness did not last. We were pushed unceremoniously into a room occupied by only two beds—two split straw mattresses covered with a disgusting sheet on which dozens of bedbugs cried out in famine. After two hours, I was completely eaten up; I jumped out the window and climbed the mountain because dogs were howling in the distance. I stopped under a tree and fell into a deep sleep—right in the middle of the Balkans! What would my mother have said had she known?

I am writing these lines from a desert island where a stupid quarantine is detaining us with some fellow sufferers for a few days. I've reached the point where I no longer count the nights spent under the stars, on the hard decks of the ships that brought us this far, or on the sands of this island made white-hot in the terrible sun which, just a few kilometers from here, also caresses the exquisite marbles of the Parthenon that I have yet to see!

# ON TURKISH SOIL

From Kazanlŭk (where, for two weeks now, the Valley of Roses has entrusted its fragrant treasures to retorts) to Stara Zagora we travel by post-horse.

We arise at three in the morning. There are six of us, who try to keep warm in an open dirty little cart, while dying to sleep. The three horses run like devils and jostle us over pitiful roads that often merge with the stream.

We overtake migrating Turkish tziganes. Tall men with turbans and variegated shirts; women covered by indigo-blue veils bordered with material the color of wine dregs. The young girls are very beautiful, much more so than their swiftly faded elder sisters. They all wear culotte skirts, the very stylish culotte skirts, simple and finely modeled. The youngsters, almost naked, are whimpering, of course. Everyone is on foot, the donkeys carry enormous bundles. The Balkans at the base of the plateau are dark blue, and the sun is not to appear today. Every now and then on the narrow road some Turk passes by on a little donkey—so small that the old man, crowned with a turban, appears gigantic; at about fifteen centimeters from the ground, his legs kick at the rate of more than sixty beats per minute, because donkeys are always trotting along while appearing to take nosedives. He is a good jackass and delightfully conscientious! And the old Turk is basically kindhearted.

Here is the first Turkish cemetery. It lies at the end of the little town where in each garden we visited, they had given us rose preserves and then with pleasant smiles had escorted us away while sprinkling us with a few drops of rosewater—rosewater from the Valley of Roses! In these courtyards water flowed from a marble fountain, and everything was covered with flowers between borders of trimmed box

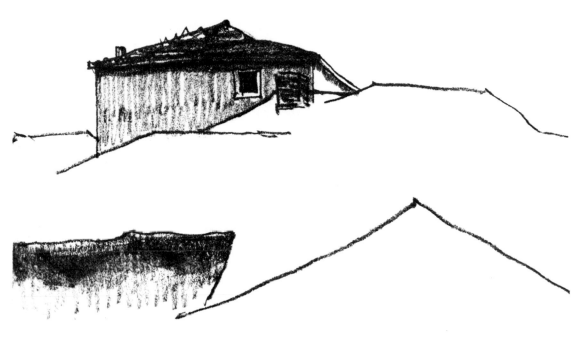

*Peasant house in Kazanlŭk*
*(courtesy Jean Petit)*

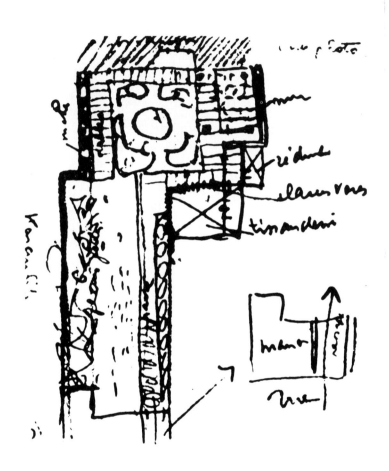

*Plan and perspective
of a house in Kazanlŭk
(courtesy FLC)*

hedges and white sandy footpaths, under a generously large vine trellis. The walls are of a blinding white, or sometimes painted with an ultramarine limewash. Thus the cemetery binds the city to the plain and makes for it a gateway of reverie. The stones bristle up from clumps of thistles like menhirs, but there are many tiny ones. They are incoherent, disordered, and uncut, without designation, without inscription, and without symbol: a fragment of elongated rock, stuck into the ground.[1] Tall, nondescript plants contribute to the impression of a strong vertical thrust on this vast plateau; their flowers are lemon yellow, the only color to be seen against the rich gray of the rough stones and the dried-up blues of the thistles. Flocks of sheep and solitary oxen graze among these overgrown grasses in this serene city of the dead.

The trains are not punctual. But all the same Auguste noticed that we had at last arrived at Adrianople, seventeen hours late. Oh! you would not believe the sudden storms and floods, or the stationmasters!

At the door, an apparition of ruffians! They jump aboard the carriage and, here we are, twelve men in this ten-seat compartment! Our ruffians, who might have been painted by Decamps,[2] are decent peasant chaps who shake their heads at the sight of thousands of golden sheaves rolling in a swell on the tempestuous yellow river. But they stink unbearably of garlic. I was given a rose at Siemen; I now press my nostrils against it. Auguste listens to my complaints; smoking his pipe, he philosophizes, and, philosophizing, he puffs on his pipe.

The scenery might have been painted by Decamps. The good man really struck the right note: a storm-blackened sky against which a mountain rises up in light ocher: the trees converge to a hard, opaque shadow, and the clouds make grim patches on the ground. It is a setting

*Courtyard with a marble*
*fountain (courtesy FLC)*

for battles. Herds of gray oxen and black buffaloes placidly enjoy the unexpected bath that the unchained Maritsa has been offering them since yesterday evening; wallowing in yellow water up to their necks, the buffaloes lift their gloomy heads and ruminate.

Adrianople[3] appears in the splendor of full afternoon light. Adrianople is like a swelling on this vast plateau, culminating in a magnificent dome. Tremendous minarets, in the distance as delicate as marsh horsetails, emphasize and direct this great thrust upright. Three other enormous and awesome mosques come to lend support to this joyous effort. The Sultan Selim gives the city a tiara of great splendor. The ancient Turkish capital has remained full of nobility. With their pure Eastern manners the fine old Turks who live here appear to us as holy men.

We were coddled, which means we were greeted by everyone and treated with kindness. In the cafés—Turkish ones, of course—the owner (*kahveci*), crouching on a sofa, gets up and with pincers brings burning charcoal taken from the oven to light our cigarettes. We are seated on the street beneath a trellis. Kindly and curious Turks become interested and gather round. A pastry vendor offers us some of his goods and refuses to be paid. I knocked over and broke two water glasses. And the *kahveci* is offended because I want to reimburse him; from his wide-open window where he smokes the narghile while crouching on a couch, he smiles, says thank you, salutes us, and won't even accept payment for the coffee.

We are wide-eyed at the new scenes that multiply across the street. Facing us, a fellow is seated in front of his house. Before him are two pots of pink geraniums. His head is shaved like that of a tonsured monk, but the razor has crept down to his forehead. It is the summer haircut of Turkish men, and it is strangely powerful.

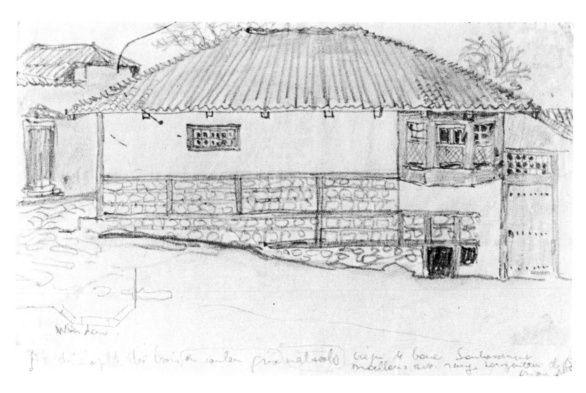

*House in Adrianople*
*(courtesy FLC)*

A companion approaches holding an immense watering can. Our fellow gets down on his knees in an attitude of worship, his head forward between the geraniums, and his faithful friend sprinkles water generously onto his head. The water flows endlessly from the huge can; the patient groans with pleasure and points now and then to the place on his skull where the sprinkling is the most agreeable. He gets up, squats down again, and, hands on his knees, waits behind the two pots of geraniums for night to fall and coolness to come. The street where we sip innumerable cups of coffee (they cost only a few cents, bless them) ascends toward the mosque of Sultan Selim, and every now and then it is covered by vine trellises spanning the road and offering joy and shade. Again, imagine here and there an ivory marble fountain or the brilliant whiteness of some pointed minaret against the tender azure of the sky.

Little donkeys go up and down the streets unbelievably overburdened and too funny for words. These small beasts always work seriously, with their whole souls. It is amusing to see how these lazy old buggers load them down, with bundles of freshly cut grass so crookedly stacked that they tumble to the ground, bringing with them an entire patch of fragrant prairie grass, or with enormous baskets filled with tomatoes, onions, and garlic. This whole bundle—the donkey, the Turk, the straw, or the tomatoes and all—is so wide that it often fills the entire street. This is probably why a laundryman, from fear of being jostled, has set up shop in a wardrobe suspended above the street under the porch of the Old Bazaar. The door panels have been replaced by glass; in his slightly uncommon dwelling the man is thus sheltered from donkeys as well as from the cold! At Kazanlŭk, a fellow tradesman had discovered how comfortable a large doghouse can be for working his leather. At his place, too, there was the luxury of glass. The old chap was

*Marble fountain (courtesy FLC)*

hunchbacked, bald, and wore thick glasses. His hut lay in the middle of the square, and beside and in front of him, chains of garlic, onions, and leeks were being sold.

We are eating in a local restaurant. Only Turks come in, calm in their great black gowns, austere under their white or green turbans. They wash their hands and mouths with soap at the marble ewer, and the owner takes a break from his stove to offer them a towel. They circulate around the cooking pots, make their choice, then solemnly come and sit down. They do not talk. In this little establishment where five four-person tables are squeezed together, there is a silence that we do not find at all oppressive. We have the feeling of being in very distinguished company.

An entire wall of this square room is made of windows that open onto the street; the ovens lean against it, and the large open bays let out aromas that spread the fame of this tavern over the whole street. Beside the ovens is a big slab of thick marble serving as a sideboard, and on it the provisions are spread out: tomatoes, cucumbers, beans, cantaloupes, and watermelons, in short all those cucurbits of which Turks are so fond. We are served a very heavy noodle soup with lemon, then some little stuffed squash,[4] and some barely cooked rice sauteed in oil. As a rule the Turks eat no meat. Limiting themselves to a vegetarian diet, they don't need knives; hence the table knife is unknown. To this very rich menu they always add a few cups of fruit juices, cherry, pear, apple, or grape, which they drink with a spoon; wine is condemned by Mohammed. The aristocratic Turks of the old regime use only their fingers and a piece of bread to eat with; they handle it with great finesse. All the while a boy, wearing a fez and girt with a woolen belt which makes him as broad as he is tall, runs from guest to guest waving a long pole crowned by an enormous mop of white paper. In the face of the uproar that he makes and the atmospheric disturbances produced by his device, the flies flee by the thousands—but, quite undeceived and quickly recovered from their terror, they soon begin their deafening round all over again.

Before setting foot on Byzantine soil, I had the privilege of enjoying, at Rodosto, an exquisite little port town perched on a hillside overlooking the Marmara, a very Turkish experience, but Turkish "new" regime!

Invited to dine at the home of some merchants I had met quite by chance, I spent the evening with them in their garden. The trump of these gentlemen was to bring down, from the shadows of a large tree, a colossal incandescent gas lamp, as huge as an arc light at the Brandenburg Gate in Potsdam Square. Eight hundred candles! they announced, and then they lit it up! We had this right over our noses, only one meter above the table. And we spoke of progress, the new constitution, and civilization.

The evening finished in music, and these gentlemen, affable as ever, went up to get their instruments—a mandolin and a guitar. A page boy covered the table with sheets of music. Then they insisted that I state my preference for serious music or frivolous music, for the waltz or the madrigal. As I could not manage to declare my preference so categorically, saying that I liked all music, they seemed displeased, and, after tuning their instruments and shuffling around innumerable musical scores for more than an hour, they spent two minutes playing a piece for me that depicted a call for retreat in a military barracks—that is, the sound of the trumpet and then drums that fade away little by little in the distance!

*"Rodosto, an exquisite little port town perched on a hillside overlooking the Marmara" (courtesy FLC)*

*Turkish house between
Murattis and Rodosto,
and at Rodosto
(courtesy FLC)*

Then they wanted to take me to what they called, simply, the "Club" (pronounced "kleube," if you will). It was on a quite beautiful terrace overlooking the sea. The moon flooded the humid plains with a blue light. From the windows of the Club, open and bursting with light, there shot forth a piercing and triumphant fanfare. We went in. It was the trade employees' brass band, founded at the advent of the Constitution. The enthusiasm of these very young and very old men, blowing like madmen into wood and brass pipes, was touching. The harmony rose up, munificient, carried on the wings of faith.

And on the wall a large oil painting depicted a life-sized and classically half-naked Orpheus, seated and weeping with his lyre. Before him, two goats, a lion in the forest, and at his feet, a rooster accompanied by a magpie and a hen. All this in the manner of Puvis de Chavanne.[5] In the garden there are beautiful antique bas-reliefs, though not exactly as they would appear to us in a museum because, in a splendid sarcophagus from the third century, bottles of lemonade were bathing in its coolness . . .

On the bedsheets at the hotel the black of the bedbugs was easily equal to the white of unwashed linen.

# CONSTANTINOPLE

Pera, Stamboul, Scutari: a trinity. I love this word, because there is something sacred about it.[1]

Papa Bonnal and I were slowly drinking resin wine on our balcony in Ainali-Tchechme—he before a late dinner, I after having dined in Stamboul and come back across the bridge.[2] From our vantage point we could see the Golden Horn beyond the cascading cypresses in the Little Fields. Below, Stamboul sits above a broad band of shadow, outlining the silhouettes of its great mosques against the darkened sky. When there is moonlight—we had it twice—the sea, visible beyond it, ties the minarets together with a shimmering thread along the gloomy ridge.

Night has fallen. I am a little giddy. Is it I who dreams, or is it my narrator carried away by his imagination? His hoarse voice rasps. His big, drunkard's eyes are moist and sparkling beneath their heavy gray eyebrows.[3] The night is yellow and trickles with gold. All the marble statuary of all the palaces of Byzantium is there, as well as all the treasures of the sultans and all the gems of the Seraglios! A solid gold Venus and a Ceres stand at the head of the Phanal, the stairway of Justinian's palace, leading down to the water. Lying in the sand at the promontory of the Seraglio are bronze cannons decorated in gold and big solid gold rings like those that they—the divine, thrilling oda-lisques—used to wear around their naked ankles and arms like serpents. Loaded with gold, their nails painted in vermillion, they suffocated from waiting so long in their magnificent cages at the apex of this hill which juts out into the sea and breaks the waves before Stamboul. And for having failed to please once, they were slid into a sack, dropped all the way down making a "plop" in the water, and little fish nibbled away their flesh. Papa Bonnal claims that their finery

*View of Pera, Stamboul,*
*and Scutari from the sea*
*(courtesy FLC)*

is all there, left behind to bear witness. Eurythmics of marble rise out of the sea and reflect in the water as they advance along the shores. Countless lilies planted everywhere prove that the marbles are gilded by the incessant sun; they spread their heavy, suffocating fragrance over polished flagstones of prophyry, malachite, verde antique, and jade, amid the sparkle of inlaid mother-of-pearl. SHE—I don't know who—I suppose some Theodora, but what does it matter as long as she wears her Ravenna finery and as long as her eyes, enlarged by a black outline, gnaw her cheeks; SHE is waiting in some exedra for the lunar blue to absorb the light of day.[4] When she leans over the edge of the wave-lapped stairs, her jewels seem to multiply, the gems taking on a hard luster that the exulting water casts back in her face. Rays of sunshine play on the wisteria hanging on the porticos and whiffs of perfume drift above the water. The sky makes a pool of fire as in an icon, and sanctifies the madness of the hour. The waves coming from the Sweet Waters of Europe follow a delicate curve. No, it's no illusion: the banks that hold them are curved like an enormous cornucopia emptying itself into the sea across Asia, whose mountains are spread out like the placid horizontal smile of a Buddha in the shadow of a sanctuary, covered by a golden luster.

But enough of this wretched yellow. Stubbornly, I swear to Papa Bonnal that this is not all there is to it. I want Stamboul to sit upon her Golden Horn all white, as raw as chalk, and I want light to screech on the surface of domes which swell the heap of milky cubes, and minarets should thrust upward, and the sky must be blue. Then we would be free of all this depraved yellow, this cursed gold. Under the bright light, I want a city all white, but the green cypresses must be there to punctuate it. And the blue of the sea shall reflect the blue of the sky.

*The Golden Horn that cuts
through Constantinople
(courtesy FLC)*

*"Under the bright light, I want a city all white, but the green cypresses must be there to punctuate it"* (courtesy FLC)

Thus did we arrive by sea like in old times, to watch all these things unfold. It was not simply a detour but also a bizarre idea that brought us bedbugs at Rodosto and thirteen hours of stormy seas in a very small boat.

Just like the Russian pilgrims who the other day were watching for the first sight of the Holy Mountain,[a] we were waiting expectantly on the upper deck when the Seven Towers appeared. Afterward came a number of small mosques, followed by large ones and then the ruins of Byzantine palaces; finally Hagia Sophia and the Seraglio appeared. We entered the Golden Horn between Pera, dominated by its Genoese Tower, and Stamboul, planted with minarets—each on a mountain facing the other. I was deeply moved, for I had come here to worship these things which I knew to be so beautiful.

The leaden sky drizzled, turning the sea gray. The Golden Horn was muddy, and its banks as unstable as a marsh. The mosques, dirty as an old wall, shaded wooden houses stacked among numerous trees. I didn't even see Scutari: it was behind us, and I forgot to look.

Sailors and stevedores cried out, and from their rowboats dancing madly back and forth they climbed aboard our little ship. We were unloaded with the same disregard one might show for cattle and found ourselves bewildered in the very middle of a street swarming with a crowd of Greeks, Germans, and French, all that suspect blend of the Levantine. There were omnibuses, and it was raining. It rained for four days, and a leprous gray stretched out over everything. For three weeks I waited for the weight on my heart to lighten. I had to work at it, and most of all I wanted to love this place.

a. Mount Athos.

As for the imperially corrupt Byzantium, I don't think it can be brought back to life. Its spirit has departed from the few stones that remain.

For three weeks I gave vent to my rancor against these things which had decked themselves out to show up at our every encounter—how shocking! Auguste too was hopping mad, and I came to ask myself in anguish whether I was not a fool for remaining so morose in the presence of Stamboul, Pera, and Scutari.

Finally, I found my road to Damascus. I came to understand this majestic Unity, and day after day I lived by its trinitarian principles. I think they are mutually indispensable to each other because their characters are profoundly dissimilar, even though they complement one another. Pera, Stamboul, Scutari, a Trinity! Ah yes, because Sweet Death has its altars everywhere and unites all hearts with the same serenity and the same hope. Yet Scutari resolutely takes refuge in the mystery of her cypresses, where thousands upon thousands of neglected tombs are covered with moss, and she leaves Pera and Stamboul facing each other beyond the Bosphorus, on European soil. Pera, perched on a mountain, overlooks Stamboul on her hills and covets her. The Golden Horn between them crouches dull and formless. But two bridges unite them, one almost abandoned, the other shaking with a feverish vitality. To bring them together even more, there are also hundreds of rowboats furtively spaced between fully inflated sailboats and the massive hulls of huge steamers whose harsh blasts are accompanied by dense black smoke, always blown toward Stamboul—because of the Bosphorus— where it flicks its dirty tongue at the naive whiteness of the poor mosques. These bridges, built on pontoons, open up at night to allow the Golden Horn to disgorge entire flotillas that formed during the day, while one by one amid cries and curses sailboats as large as those of Ulysses fold their sails, bend their masts, and slip between the pontoons. To the left and right they have formed two forests of masts, rocked by the movement of water or rendered motionless as minarets by the killing light of midday.

The Middle East centers around a formidable tower at Pera, a compressed city with the allure of New York, enclosing Turks who doze into an indefatigable *kef.* Wooden houses with large spread-out roofs warm their purple colors amidst fresh greenery and within enclosures whose mystery delights me;[5] although they group themselves quite harmoniously around all these summits formed by really enormous mosques, a poisoned atmosphere hangs over Pera, under an unrelenting light. Stone houses scale up within, thrusting upward like upright dominoes, offering two sections of white walls riddled with windows and then two adjoining walls the color of dried blood. Nothing softens the severity of this height. There are no trees, for they would take too much space. The streets rise crazily and leave breathless these people already made breathless by their thirst for gain; the houses join upper stories over extremely narrow streets. There is a lot of cohesion, even competition, within this feverish activity, so much so that it brings about not only a sense of unity, but also beauty. And that Pera—awesome, arid, dried-up and heartless, a pitiless, anonymous pile of rocks like Messina in ruins—that Pera is beautiful and imposing, with its huge round tower resembling both a fortress of war and a bellicose watchtower standing as arrogantly as a *condottier.*[6]

No church steeples jut out of it, nor are there any ringing bells here. Whom would they call to devotions? Here rather are devotees of pleasure. They are absorbed in making themselves beautiful, and sometimes they appear chic. Ah! But they don't succeed like those in Bucharest!

*The Pera skyline with its
formidable Genoese Tower
(courtesy FLC)*

The stone houses of Pera
climbing the hillside (courtesy FLC)

The quays on the Golden Horn are squalid, and the entrance to the new bridge is precarious: the streets tumble into it like the slanted lines of a funnel toward its bottleneck. So the crowds jostle and shout at each other! We exchange blows back and forth, and then on the bridge we are engulfed in a dense and brutal mass which is difficult to channel on account of the patrol of white-coated tolltakers with brutal[7] faces who stretch out their hands to fill their double sacks shouting, grimacing, and becoming completely disheveled because of this ugly trade that hardens their hearts and makes their hands greasy from the filth of coins.

All that commotion by the cramped water's edge is Galata, the seaward quarter, with its houses drawn together in a common stench. The population of dockworkers and sea merchants[8] drink resin wine, sell fish, and eat their food with garlic. There the banks build hotels, the shipping companies their agencies, and the customs house its offices.[9] Pushed into Stamboul, we still feel the effects of this foul rush for another quarter of an hour. The streets prostitute themselves, disowning their centuries of Turkish life and selling their favors to greedy merchants; even the temples of Allah are besmirched.[10] And then we climb and get away. We enter streets lined with cemeteries and *türbes,*[b] and we find peace beside a fountain as beautiful as a temple, guarded by a cypress. We turn into little streets sectioned off by large wooden houses, *konaks,* or simple dwellings, connected one to another by high garden walls. Along the curve of the street we see nothing but two high walls, as pink as salmon meat. We are nevertheless perfectly

b. Monumental burial sepulchers of the sultans. (Editor's note: This and the following three footnotes by Jeanneret date from 1911.)

happy, reflecting on the joyful life that goes on behind some fifty centimeters of brick and stone—a life of day-dreaming in carefully sequestered gardens. Prisons, perhaps, but the prisons of odalisques. For us at this moment it felt like a slightly painful, melancholic, beneficent poem.

Upon the hilltops of Stamboul the shining white "Great Mosques" swell up and spread themselves out amid spacious courtyards surrounded by neat tombs in lively cemeteries. The *hans*[c] make them a tight army of little domes, and the cypresses standing alone in the deserted courtyard join to the playful motion of minarets the black austerity of their rigid and long-suffering silhouettes; their grooved trunks reveal how venerable they are. I would like to say something about the Turkish soil, but I will not succeed! There is here an unbounded serenity. We call it fatalism to disparage it: we should call it "faith." A faith that I would describe as pink—or rather pink and blue, blue because the horizontal of the sea is blue and because the sky is blue. Here one never sees where the one ends and the other begins. As such, it is a boundless, radiant faith.

I myself, alas, have known only an agonizing faith, which accounts for the goodwill I feel toward those people back there. (I say "back there" because we had to leave them, because I am sick, and the ship is headed for Brindisi—on the return voyage!) But what of their sharp eyes and their noses like eagles' beaks? They are the omens of storms suddenly bursting into cyclones. The sight of their outbursts and unrestrained rage can be awesome! In the depths of their rosy souls there burrows a dangerous and painful hydra. Too much serenity leads to suffering from melancholy. That's what I really wanted to say. I saw them

c. Vast stone structures surrounding most mosques.

speechless amid "fatal" flames: Stamboul was burning like a demonic offering. I heard them in their poignant mysticism before Allah, such hope! And I adored everything about them: their muteness and rigid expressions, their supplication to the Unknown, and the mournful credo of their beautiful prayers. Then during the moonlit evenings and black nights of Stamboul my ear was filled by the swooning of their souls and those undulating recitals of all the *muezzins*[d] on their minarets when they chant and call the devoted to prayer! Immense domes enclose the mystery of closed doors, minarets soar triumphantly skyward; against the whitewash of high walls dark green cypresses shake their tops as rhythmically and solemnly as they have done for centuries. A little patch of the sea is always in view. Eagles hover overhead, tracing perfect circles over the geometry of the mosques and inscribing in space immense and horizontal imaginary discs. On the masonry obelisk of the Hippodrome, at this vibrant hour, facing the Mosque of Ahmet, an eagle is almost always up there on some stone refuge; he looks over his black shoulder, not at the *muezzins* on the ten minarets but beyond them at Asia—all blue but at the same time reddish-brown because of the distance—with its boundless mountains that appear so seductive.

Inside each mosque they pray and chant. Having washed their mouths, faces, hands, and feet, they prostrate themselves before Allah, their foreheads striking the mats; with loud laments they cry out in the ritual rhythms of worship. On his rostrum overlooking the expanse of the nave, crouched, upright, and facing the ground with his hands in a worshipful gesture, the imam responds to the imam of the *mirhab* who leads the prayer.[11] Foreigners are forced out pitilessly. Many times,

d. Eunuchs attached to the mosque who call the faithful to prayer from the top of the minarets.

however, I was able to observe these devotions, crouched in the shadow of a niche and perhaps because of the perfectly happy look that I could not conceal. At this very moment there are millions of them throughout Islam facing toward the black Kaaba in Mecca with open arms. At the moment when all foreheads radiate the same adoration, boundless horizons bite into the bloody disc of the sun. The fire crier's custom says all of its tragic soul in the black of moonless nights.

Stamboul is a closely knit agglomeration; every mortal's dwelling is of wood, every dwelling of Allah is of stone. I have already said that it hangs against the side of this great hill like a suspended carpet of violet wool blended with tints of emerald; the mosques on the crests are its prestigious fasteners. Here there are only two types of architecture: the big flattened roofs covered with worn tiles and the bulbs of the mosques with minarets shooting up. They are linked to each other by cemeteries.

When there is a fire in overcrowded Stamboul, it is terrible. Criers walk the streets at night, tapping on the hard stone pavement with heavy iron rods. That noise, in all its solemnity, is the same sound that parts the crowds beneath the vaults of Notre-Dame in Paris to make way for the holy prelates or for the sacred utensils at holy communion. Almost every night there is a fire. If the wind is blowing—or if some underhanded revenge is involved—Stamboul is consumed. It is atrocious, awesome. It is a gigantic candelabrum that we, Europeans, are watching with looks of terror. As for them, they let the flames spread, persuaded that these things are predetermined. Then in complicity with the night the Turkish soul resigns itself; the lights remain out and no one stays up to watch. There is a silence that only one who has *heard* it can imagine.

*Kasim-Pasha (courtesy
FLC)*

Very far away our nervous ears detect the impact of metal on the paving stones of the street, and suddenly out of the jet-black darkness there bursts the agonizing shriek of a dying man struck by some treacherous blow, still crying out in horror. It lasts a long time, several seconds. It reverberates with an Eastern rhythm like the verses of an ancient Greek chorus—then it dies out in a death rattle. The night and the silence renew their bond of complicity until at the corner of a house metal unexpectedly clangs against stone, and the disturbing lament rings out once again. The man cries out that there is a fire in such and such a place. And, if there are any relatives of the victims, they dress quickly, push open the wooden door, and slip out into the labyrinth of blind alleys crowned by the darkness of trees.

In counterpoint, by fits and starts, far off to the right and left, all the way down to the edge of the sea, and farther into Kasim-Pasha, the same cry springs forth like a spurt of blood. Carried up by the slender cypresses, it rises, causing those asleep in the *konaks*[e] to shudder with fear. Because of the fire four lights have been lit in the huge round Genoese Tower in Pera. Facing them, on the crest of Stamboul, the Seraskie fire tower hangs out two lights. Thus it is made known to everyone, those on the Marmara and those on the Golden Horn, those is Aksaray and in Tophané, and even those in their cemeteries in Scutari, that there is a fire and that Stamboul once again is crumbling. It is said that the city sheds its skin in this way every four years! Behind their belt of *hans* the great mosques remain invincible. In the caress of the flames they shine like alabaster, more mystical than ever, the invulnerable temples of Allah!

e. Name given to Turkish houses.

*View of Stamboul with its enclosing walls and great mosques (courtesy FLC)*

# THE MOSQUES

It must be a silent place facing toward Mecca. It needs to be spacious so that the heart may feel at ease, and high so that prayers may breathe there. There must be ample diffused light so as to have no shadows; the whole should be perfectly simple; and a kind of immensity must be encompassed by the forms. The floor must be more spacious than a public square, not to contain great crowds but so that the few who come to pray may feel joy and reverence within this great house. Nothing should be hidden from view: one enters and sees the immense square covered with golden mats of rice straw, always new, and no furnishings or seats but only a few lecterns close to the ground bearing copies of the Koran before which one kneels. At a glance one sees the four corners, distinctly feels their presence and then construes the great cube perforated by small windows from which spring the four gigantic transverse arches uniting the pendentives; then one sees the crown sparkling with the thousand tiny windows of the dome. Overhead is a vast space whose size one cannot grasp, for the half sphere has the unique charm of eluding measurement. From above hang innumerable wires; they almost reach the ground to hold rods on which the little oil lamps are hung, a crystalline procession turning in concentric circles, which in the evening suspends a luminous ceiling over the heads of the faithful; within the encircling band of windows now dimmed, never-ending wires climb toward the top of the dome and disappear in the obscurity of that immense space.

The *mihrab,* facing the entrance, is no more than a door to the Kaaba. It has neither protrusions nor depth.

All these things are clothed in a majestic coat of whitewash. The forms stand out clearly; the impeccable construction displays all its boldness. At times a high stylobate of delightful ceramic produces a blue vibration.

*The Mosque of Suleyman*
*(courtesy FLC)*

*Interior of a mosque*
*(courtesy FLC)*

The Young Turks have been ashamed of the simplicity of their fathers, and consequently, all the mosques in Turkey, with the exception of Bursa, which was rescued by Loti, have suffered the ignominy of repugnant and revolting painted ornamentation.[1] Yes, as I have said, to love them despite all of this requires hard work and commitment. In front of the sanctuary there must be a marble-paved courtyard surrounded by a portico; pointed arches supporting small domes descend upon verde antique porphyry columns. Under this portico there are three portals, one opening to the north, one to the south, and another to the east. The water temple used for the ablutions is in the center, with its charming roof in the form of a kiosk and its twenty or forty open spigots set in marble panels below an enormous cylindrical basin that stands higher than a man. Viewed from outside, the high walls of the court form a forbidding prism of ashlar; there the three portals open beneath a cascade of stalactites. This prism is like the feet of the giant sphinx suggested by the outline of the mosque as it stands at night on the crest of Stamboul.[2]

And then there must be a parvis, an open gravelly area with a few cypresses. Paved paths lead to the doors of the mosque and toward a cemetery overgrown with age-old plane trees.[3] This cemetery is a counterpart to the courtyard at the other side of the sanctuary. A wall of cut stone, perforated with a thousand openings through its latticework, closes off the streets lined with caravansaries. Monumental portals as large as houses open directly onto the paved paths of the courtyard. The caravansaries form a rigid quadrangle all around. A multitude of little lead domes line up on their terraced roofs. These domes are centered, measured, and proportioned in relation to the sanctuary to which they belong. They enclose the schools of the imams around courtyards shaded by arcades rich with flowers and trellises, in addition to the caravansaries with their superimposed double porticoes animated by the murmur of fountains. Flanking the sanctuary, there must be minarets so tall as to carry afar the shrill voices of the *muezzins* chanting and calling the devoted to prayer at hours regulated by the sun. Impressive notes filter down from above. The city of wood lies all around. Within its own city of stones, the white sanctuary raises its dome atop great cubes of masonry.

An elementary geometry orders these masses: the square, the cube, the sphere. In plan it is a rectangular complex with a single axis. The orientation of the axis of every mosque on Moslem soil toward the black stone of the Kaaba is an awe-inspiring symbol of the unity of the faith.

One evening at the far end of Stamboul near the "Great Walls,"[4] exhausted by so many comings and goings, I saw the dome and minarets of the Mosque of Sultan Selim[a] glowing in the murky twilight. I went toward it. In the streets, also tired from the day's swarming, the last Turks watched me pass by with astonishment: at sunset, Stamboul becomes again wholly Turkish. People from Pera say, "Be careful, don't go there, don't stay there; they are barbarians, they will kill you!" I walked along a street overlooking vast vegetable gardens, then came the caravansaries, the wall, the open space with a few cypresses, and then tombs encircled by enclosures leaning against the mosque, and there are *türbes*[b] too, as large as baptisteries. A high embankment wall plunges into the shadows, the Golden Horn loses its form in the night. And against the sky there is the black row of the great mosques. In

a. It is one of the great mosques of Istanbul.
b. *Türbes* are large tombs built for important personages.

*A monumental portal in
the enclosing wall of the
Mosque of Suleyman.
(courtesy FLC)*

*The prism of the Mosque of Suleyman, "like the feet of the giant Sphinx" (courtesy FLC)*

*The great white Mosque of*
*Sultan Selim (courtesy FLC)*

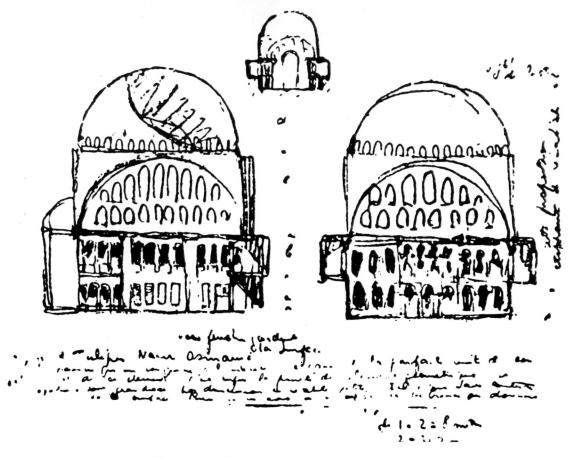

*The geometry of a mosque
in cross section: "the square,
the cube, the sphere."
Nuruosmaniye Mosque
(courtesy FLC)*

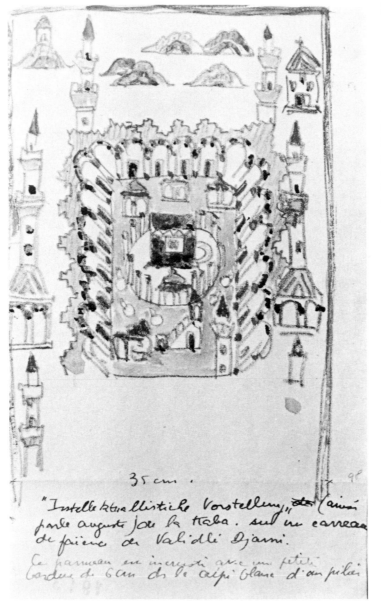

the courtyard the bubbling of the water temple cannot be heard beyond the cloud of shadows descending from the domed porticoes.

A few men with long dark robes are performing their ablutions; then one after another, walking across the marble pavement under the canopy of stalactites, they lift up by a corner the heavy portiere surbased with leather and red velvet.

There is in the sky, before the night hardens things, a watershed of emerald green and indigo blue. It seems as if the great round bellies of the domes are casting off the heat they have absorbed: these forms glow, green within a darker green, like a majestic disc flanked by two shafts above the square of the porticoes.

The portiere fell back. A ceiling of stars was spread out in concentric rings over the people in prayer. It was rather like a soft gauze formed by the flickering of a thousand tiny night lamps, which made the four square walls of the sanctuary seem inordinately far away. The pious murmur rose ever higher into the forest of suspended wires where it faded away in the bosom of the dome. This fictitious ceiling of light, three meters above the mats, and the immense shadowy space that swells above it, are one of the most poetical architectural creations known to me.

Bare-footed, the faithful line up in various places in the nave and prostrate often, all together. Having waited for long-lasting seconds with heads bowed to the ground, then upright with eyes beholding the *mihrab* and hands folded in worship, they would repeat, "Allah," in a deep voice after the imam's utterance from the gallery. Then someone among the gathering began to sing a credo in a sharp head voice as used in liturgy; the sounds, modulated along a horizontal line, were emitted in sudden spurts and then fell back mournfully, terribly sorrowful and melancholic. Then, the faithful rose and left.

*The skyline of Stamboul*
*with its black row of great*
*mosques (courtesy FLC)*

*Water temple set in an enclosing wall (courtesy FLC)*

There were still a few of them in the darkness when I went out. One of them approached me and shook my hand; he laughed at himself because of our inability to communicate with each other and because I looked so perplexed. The others came over, and some of them also shook my hand. I left them and walked away toward the bridge. I knew I would have to walk two hours to reach home, but I was happy in a silence filled with these things.

The ashlar enclosures of cemeteries border this path, revealing through their openings the sleep of so many tombs. How profuse are the water temples here, whose fine-crafted beauty was ordained by the sultan donor who instituted the gift of water so that he might be venerated for all eternity! Here come the quadrangles of the caravansaries, and the "Sultan Mehmet" with two rococo minarets and a huge dome, and then a gate closing off the courtyard.[5] Two *türbes* or a single one, seen in this prismatic form, mark the place where a sultan lies beneath in his brocades and surrounded by the coffins of his wives; and then again cemetery walls appear. The aqueduct, a Byzantine specter, blackens the darkness of the night, modern with its long form resembling a liner riddled with portholes.[6] It leans against the Shehzade, a strange mosque dominating several large tombs.[7]

I met no one. A few streetlamps illuminated a huge marble wall whose golden patina was punctuated by arcades. Here and there bronze gates wove their complicated spiderwebs; cypresses rise up above the wall. Pressing my face against the metal bars, I could discern tombs. Occasionally, an opening on the left would show lights reflecting off patches of water in the Golden Horn; sometimes the sparkle of the Marmara could be seen to the right. On a rise, in the middle ground, was the sphinxlike apparition of the colossal Mosque of Suleyman, the work of that man who built almost a hundred of them, and I don't know how many caravansaries.[8] *Türbes* were interspersed with an occasional school—no doubt a gift—and the road continued between darkened arcades where, by day, the whole noisy turbulence of Turkish life spreads out on the streets.

The dead were sleeping to the left, then to the right, and further on—on both sides. Some sultans have illuminated the interiors of their sober and often beautiful shrines with glazed tiles. Soon, Bayazit, the Mosque of the Doves, appeared with its minarets standing exceptionally far apart and intersecting the Grand Bazaar, whereas Nuruosmaniye, the Mosque of the Tulips, stands as its counterpart.[9] One can perceive its minarets, pale and distant, and its walls all spruced up in a strange rococo style. The Burnt Column, Byzantine in style but on a Turkish pedestal, projects into the air its porphyry shaft, once shattered by the heat of fire but now held together by iron rings.[10]

A few cafés, already of a commonplace European style, and with Viennese chairs, were still open. I was approaching the end of my walk; Hagia Sophia was about to close this unique avenue that had been so impressively opened a few hours earlier, against a luminous sky, by Mihrimah Pasha, the "clumsy one," the "one-without-minarets," posed like an imperious monolith above the huge crenelated ramparts[11] of Hagia Sophia, the Byzantine church with its four added minarets. One can see the huge Mosque of Ahmed Pasha with its six minarets when standing at the edge of the ancient Hippodrome. The street turned suddenly; the bridge was not far away. Pera appeared in stark outline. Because it was late, the hovels of Galata seemed to be sleeping. I was tired and climbing slowly in the brown dust of the Little Fields. I was stumbling on marble turbans, poor decapitated ones.[12] And all

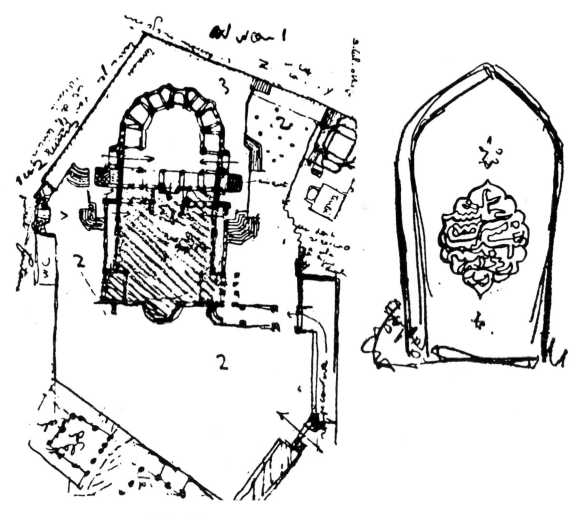

Plan of Nuruosmaniye
Mosque (courtesy FLC)

*Hagia Sophia, "the Byzan-*
*tine church with its four*
*added minarets" (courtesy*
*FLC)*

*Hagia Sophia, detail*
*(courtesy FLC)*

of a sudden, the lights from the large cafés burst forth; places where so many people seek distraction in the pleasant, affected, light, and unfailing music of Puccini.

But my path took me away from this place bereft of houses overlooking the Fields of the Dead, where cypresses are perishing from too much dust. Then, turning around before stepping over the threshold of our house, I could see all the great mosques that are standing on this huge humped back of Stamboul from the clumsy Mihrimah to the nearly excommunicated Ahmet.[c] A fog hovered over the Golden Horn, which toward dawn would thicken and flood Pera and Stamboul, but not the invulnerable ones, the mosques. Their base submerged in this sea of cotton—each one isolated within its own synthetic mass, outlined against a pallid dawn sky. Almost every evening they thrust against the ultramarine sky their majestic silhouettes.

c. The Sultan Ahmet, by building six minarets for his mosque, aroused the religious wrath of the people, for only the Kaaba at Mecca had that number. He cleverly evaded this difficulty by erecting, at his own expense, a seventh minaret at Kaaba.

*Majestic silhouettes of the mosques on the "huge humped back of Stamboul" (courtesy FLC)*

# THE SEPULCHERS

I am writing these notes from a noisy café in Athens. In front of the terrace some poor devil has set up a phonograph and is waiting for his gutta-percha records to stop playing so that he can start taking up a collection, which will bring him nothing; everywhere the music of His Master's Voice haunts this place! From the corollalike amplifier come the songs and chants of the East, one litany beginning with a shout proclaiming "I am alive!" sustained at a high pitch for a long time and continuing in descending modulations, soon weary, repeatedly falling, and dying away on a final sustained note, held as long as possible until the effort gives out.

This unexpectedly brings me back—first, to the boat where all of us who slept on deck in the open air enjoyed endless nocturnes strummed on *theorbos* and sung in head voice.[1] The pyramid of Athos was disappearing into the Virgin's colors, uniformly blue in the silver of the moon.[a] The phonograph's litanies carry me back again, to a reality that is already diffused—to Stamboul at night and Stamboul at noon, at the time of prayers. If, some happy day, I should hear such languid music again, I shall become incurably nostalgic.[2] Although restless at times, I had felt much better in the midst of the dead lying scattered about there, the most recently deceased together with their ancestors, under innumerable cypresses. There was a forest of tombstones, so old that their marble was disappearing under the lichens. Those in Stamboul are the same as those in Scutari, and those in Scutari are like those in Adrianople, the Balkans, Asia Minor, and elsewhere, I imagine.

a. Athos is the holy mountain which for more than a thousand years has been consecrated to the Virgin by the Orthodox Church. (Editor's note: This and the following two notes date from 1911.)

*Eyüp, "where tombs come*
*right onto the street"*
*(courtesy FLC)*

*Courtyard surrounded by*
*an iron grill (courtesy FLC)*

Stamboul is submerged in tombs. Everyone loves them. The tombs extend right into the courtyards of the houses. One Turkish Sunday[b] I saw a fellow through a chink in a gate, seated in his garden, his back against the white column of a tomb; he was just daydreaming, apparently not thinking of anything in particular, but, as for me, I was struck by this. Upon the pavement in the little courtyards of many residences in Rodosto and elsewhere I had already seen little lanterns at the very threshold of the doors keeping vigil over the household dead. Constantinople is a kind of wilderness; people build houses, plant trees, and where there is any space left, they bury their dead. The tombs come right onto the streets, settle under the foliage and rival the big *türbes* in which the sultans lie within the walled enclosures of the mosques; and blue thistles bloom all over this soil.

The life of the Turk passes from the mosque to the cemetery by way of the café where he smokes in silence. It is a stroke of good fortune for these proper cafés—which extend right up to the edge of the parvis—to enclose within their own courtyards, on a mound surrounded by an iron grill, the sepulcher of some saint. Every night for centuries a lamp has burned, illuminating the marble turban which occasionally receives a new coat of red or green paint, causing the gold of the exquisitely interlaced epitaph to shine.

Stamboul does not extend beyond its tremendous Byzantine walls but crams itself into spaces that are too confined. Nowadays, however, with all the spaces on the inside taken, Stamboul buries her dead in the Big Cemeteries just beyond the walls. Starting at the Golden Horn,

b. The Turks' holy day is Friday when the flag with a crescent on a purple background may be seen flying above the buildings. The Israelites' holy day is Saturday, and that of the Orthodox Christians is Sunday.

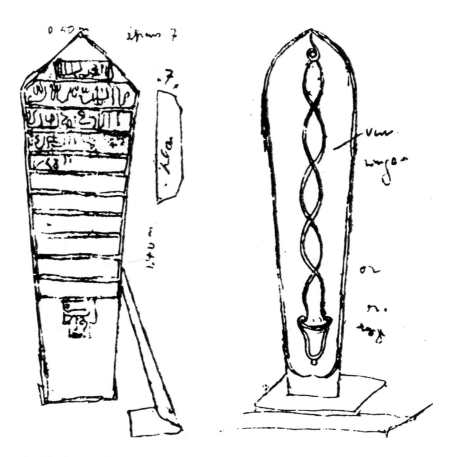

*Details of two tombstones
in Scutari, "a forgotten
necropolis in the dust"
(courtesy FLC)*

they mount the hill, and then, facing the sea,[3] slope down toward her again for some distance, blue with thistles and bristling with tombs, with great cypresses forming long avenues. Sometimes the fog comes in quite early, and then it becomes sad. It seems as if bluish blood pours over the flooded horizon. From the great walls of Byzantium, faded by defeat, appears hard and implacable the line up of enormous square towers, and that arouses anguish in my giaour's heart.[c] They see this without uneasiness because they have a religion that doesn't make them fear death.

That evening I went from Ayvan Saray up to Topkapu.[4] The view there is marvelous because one can see at a glance the entire ramparts in a vast depression with moats and enormous banks; several chariots could run abreast behind the battlements. Entire donjons have collapsed in whole blocks right into the moat.

Some women are squatting on these antique ruins; in their black hoods they look like harpies. There is one here and two over there. A harsh autumnal austerity reigns among the fog-shrouded cypresses. The fog makes everything under these skies, with their unwieldy sheathing, appear brutal. Frightened, I feel the turbulent north wind carrying the night. Its gloom spreads even among these women clinging to the bricks of old Byzantium. The folds of their capes frame their heads and then fade away below their hips, giving them the appearance of impassive bats. They remind me of those fiends at the towers of Notre-Dame. They look motionless toward the great fields bristling with tombs.[5]

Scutari is but a forgotten necropolis in the dust. Eyüp is a sacred place.[6] I think one would love to have his last sleep on this steep hill that

c. A contemptuous name given by Turks to Christians.

*The sacred burial ground
of Eyüp (courtesy FLC)*

overlooks these venerated tombs. From here one can see the Sweet Waters, the entire Golden Horn, and Asia off in the distance. When one goes back down the ancient paved way between the mounds crowned with tombstones, one encounters kindly Turks returning to their shanties up there. Up ahead, the sanctuary is already in shadow. From there one can see the dome only from above, and in the courtyard marvelous tiles make a regal entrance to that inner resting place, with so many *türbes* and sacred tombs that women make pilgrimages to it throughout the day, to whisper to the dead endless prayers and interminable meditations. Afterward, out of piety, they give blind men packages of corn to throw to the countless doves that surround the dome in a cloud of wings.

# SHE'S AND HE'S[1]

With the same moist eyes with which I worship a cat, a Persian miniature, and those bronze statuettes from Cambodia, I worship the young women and the little donkeys of Stamboul; I find between them certain affinities and resemblances.[2] I feel that I am in an aristocratic milieu: a cat, a little lady, and the little donkeys from Stamboul create beauty every moment of their lives (forgive me if I go too far in including the latter!). A Persian miniature shows us Raphael ("beloved by everyone") as coarse as rye bread. At the Musée Guimet there is a bronze Siva which I secretly caressed with my fingers, yes, for the sake of the same kind of thrill which we may experience when we dare a word or a gesture toward someone we adore, who excites us and to whom we must express it.[3]

At this moment, I am rolling along from Brindisi to Naples across the plain of Taranto, and in the compartment there are beautiful, strong, enormous Italian women. Last night, between Corfu and Brindisi across the Adriatic, I slept on deck with a cat on my stomach like a hot water bottle. By one of those fantasies of thought I suddenly recalled a Persian miniature snatched up weeks ago from one of the bandits in the Stamboul bazaar. In it a man has carried off his mistress: he has lifted the black charger that carries her and placed it on his shoulders and clutches its feet in his hands; behind him are red rocks over which he leaps like a madman; as for her, she seems dreamy, one hand to her mouth, the other holding the saddle.

Such associations of incongruous ideas conjure up contrasts, analogies, and then deductions! It is not as incoherent as it may seem! I believe that the back, belly, and head of the little donkeys of Stamboul are the artwork of a Persian painter, and that those ladies—hidden treasures in burgundy, blue, and ebony silk, who run furtively in alleyways or rest along the banks of the Sweet Waters or beneath the plane trees of Beykoz, are just as exquisite as Persian cats.[4] And if I were to speak of the beauty of their faces—which can be discovered—I should allude to the Far East, to Cambodia, less wholesome and a little less appropriate with its alabaster sculptures painted vermillion and black. I reserve the ravishing forms of Siva to describe the little donkeys, my favorites.

They won me over from the first moment—because one starts with simple things. As for the women, I hated them for three weeks not wanting to grant them anything at all! When I think now, what didn't I do then to curse them! But one day, returning home after seeing the triumphal joy of white mosques, I remarked to Klip (Klip is Auguste):

—There is some sunshine over there! And the young ladies, my dear Klip, are charming in their mysterious black veils, their disquieting anonymity of identical silks, their hidden treasures all alike. Now it seems to me they are ravishing despite and also because of that second skirt flung over their heads, that makes an impenetrable veil. You will find real coquettes underneath. I bet you, you old bony fakir, that almost all of them are young, adorable, with ivory cheeks a little full and with the innocent eyes of gazelles—delicious! After all, these veils conceal a penetrable mystery. It seems to me that there are thousands of them who wish to display their beauty, and devilish as they are, they know how to get around all the codes. They have a touch of genius: slaves of a despotic custom—maybe a wise one—which we have declared ugly and humiliating: they accomplish the miracle of revealing their individualities in attires that show no differences of cut, style, without embroidery or any combinations that could have displayed a personal fancy. How do they manage it? Simply because they have the will to appear pretty, and thereby they perform their first womanly duty—quite to the contrary of those in your province, Klip, Flemish Auguste!

—And those from yours? he retorts.

If I were to tell you more about those dear little hidden treasures, I would have to make it up. Because here we are in the realm of the inaccessible, even for so handsome a giaour as Theophile Gautier, but not so for Mr. Loti: for a person who wears a French officer's braids, lives at Tarabya, and commands a frigate, it is altogether possible that someone would be impressed with him![5]

My only adventure was this: during a fair at the entrance of Shehzade market, I was arguing vehemently with an old Turkish woman (who does not belong in this chapter) about the little printed fabrics that ordinary women wear over their heads. As I was getting angry over her exorbitant prices, a voice to one side said:

—*Sprechen Sie Deutsch?*

She was one of those little ladies. A cherry-red hidden treasure behind her black mask. She saved me from the claws of the old lady: I got my little fabrics. Then, very politely, she said:

—*Guten Tag, mein Herr!*

And she disappeared with her negro governess. A crowd of Turks on the large staircase that overlooked us stared with wide-open eyes. It was not, it seems, acceptable for a giaour to speak to a veiled lady in the very heart of Stamboul.

Take it a little further and they will lynch you like a negro in the United States. The Turk does not trifle with such matters, and you know that deep within him slumbers a hydra. As for me, I was as much delighted as disturbed! It would be superfluous for me to tell you that she was young and exquisite and that during our entire conversation I admired her through her veil. But those to whom I wrote some banal cards that evening knew that I had talked to a divine little thing and that, for a long time to come, I would remain stupefied.[6]

As for "he's" . . . but no, let's forget them for the time being, so that you may enjoy seeing for a few seconds more, between the high walls as pink as salmon, covered with lush greenery, lined with cypresses, these little silky hidden treasures at times blue, more often burgundy or ebony, who run furtively from a door that closes behind them, toward a door that will open shortly.

As for "he's," they are innumerable and of all occupations: messengers, but not swift enough for some Turks with restless ideas; carriers of debris roped all together along the steep paths of Pera like a chain of tourists on a glacier, two baskets are balanced from each side of their backs. For just one cubic meter of debris it takes about twenty-eight baskets, which raises the cost of residential excavation considerably. They also carry bricks held by a rope, and their small bells chime like a carillon. Docile, they sweat following an escort who is as brown as tobacco, and who addresses them with all kinds of speeches. Always at a trot, they carry tomatoes shining in the foliage of the vine, or heavy *carpous*,[a] with a delightful fragrance. In short, one sees them everywhere; they are an entire population between Pera and Stamboul.

Their patron is Saint Modestus: the Church has given them one so as to wrest their souls from the Turk in a fervor of proselytization. Their holiday is celebrated on Mount Athos. On such days mules and young donkeys are not whipped. Rolling in the meadows, heels up, they bray

a. A kind of melon that constitutes the staple Turkish food during the summer.

for joy; I can imagine this unusual concert. Afterward they receive double rations of feed, so much so that their pretty bellies sag, with their skin, which is so finely shaded in white, gray, and brown, then stretched tight as a drum. Saint Modestus is a saint's name which came surely from Heaven or the Academy because it is happy and perfectly suitable, but you can't understand it because you have never seen the adorable servants of this sympathetic patron saint. They know how to trot with poise and thoughtfulness, without ever raising their heads up high even though the big glass beads of turquoise, carnelian, and white glass suspended on their foreheads could make them conceited. Their lower lips hang full of gentleness, clean and neat, with a few sparse hairs strewn as on glove leather, and they carry out these difficult tasks with drawing room manners. Add a Persian robe and big black eyes—like "she's."[7]

# A CAFÉ

I entered it by chance: I was fleeing anywhere to escape the Bazaar. Everything is cool and quiet, for age-old trees mask the sky. Huge gray, red, or white striped linens are suspended from their four corners to tree trunks, and their bellies sag to within a few meters of the ground. The foliage diffuses circles of white light that dance upon the grayish patterns of irregularly shaped paving stones. Luxurious little wicker cages in which two divans face each other and, where the coffee is prepared, form on one side an uninterrupted boundary. Turkish houses block the view threading its way into the narrowness of a winding street. To get there, I climbed an odd stone stairway and went through a pretty gate in a high wall. Numerous benches are strewn about, creating enclosures; carpets of red, black, and yellow stripes cover them. They are deep and have a back and armrests. Yet they are not used for sitting down. After taking off one's shoes, one sits on one's heels. In this way one assumes a very dignified position, very neat, and this does away with our own casual habit of slouching like young revelers. The coffee is served, as you know, in tiny cups, and the tea in pear-shaped glasses. Either one costs a sou, which permits refills.

A hundred Turks converse in low voices.[1] The water gurgles in the narghiles, and the air turns blue from the smoke. We are in the land of exquisite tobaccos, and we make extravagant use of it. Only when it is out of control do we moderate it, but Auguste practically kills himself with it. Fezzes are mixed with turbans, and the long black robes with grays and blues. Here comes an old man dressed entirely in pink, which makes him look like a small child. The old people are always personable, gay, sharp-eyed, yet never helpless; prayer provides them with such health because of the exercise it requires. So these

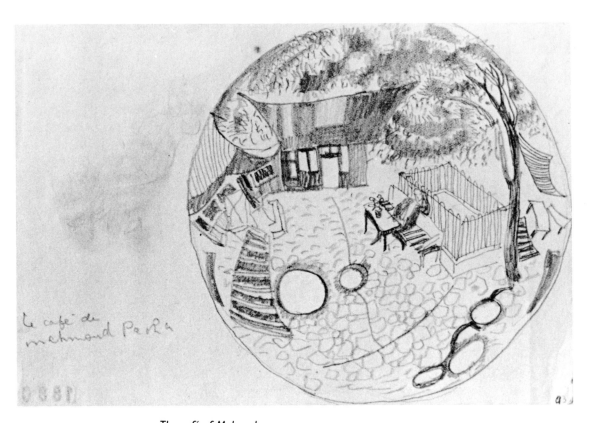

*The café of Mahmud
Pasha, near the bazaar
where Jeanneret and Klip-
stein spent many evenings
(courtesy FLC)*

old men always smile and slip by like ferrets with some inseparable *carpous* under their arms.

Over my table bloom copious blue hydrangeas; elsewhere there are roses and carnations; only two steps away I can hear the singing of a little marble fountain in Turkish rococo. Cats strut about in quest of balls of yarn, and to give you the soul of this café, I must say that the immense porch of a mosque rests its six polygonal pillars in the very midst of the benches. The capitals are carved in a very strange Spanish baroque style. Five small domes lead to an adjoining high wall, which is pierced by a high narrow door in black wood where ivory and mother-of-pearl inlays shine in a complicated linear design. Bright-colored carpets spread to the rush mats beneath the domes. The *muezzin* has just climbed the minaret which can be seen through the foliage, and his strident call to prayer pours out, while the mats are covered by the faithful who prostrate themselves, rise, and worship Allah.

But here is a touching note characteristic of the lofty, poetic Turkish soul: among the tables are three mounds, each a few meters high and bordered by a stone wall with a fine iron railing; a lantern hung to some tree which had sprouted there burns every night to illuminate the tombstones whose worn inscriptions no doubt recall the virtues of brave men now resting between the roots of the great sycamore which rises like their soul to heaven.[2] They must rest here among the living, so as to familiarize them with Sweet Death.[3] All these good old men, so nice in their childlike robes of pink, blue, or white, will come every morning to greet them and to whisper in their beards:

—Yes, yes, soon, we are coming, we are coming. I rejoice! . . .

This place, the café of Mahmud Pasha and the little mosque with a minaret and one single large dome that rests on four bare walls, is not far from the feverish Bazaar. Auguste and I spent many evenings there.

# SESAME

The Bazaar! The worst horrors are to be found in there, such as the souvenirs for tourists in all their detestable forms made to appear expensive at no cost to the merchants. They sell these wares at outrageous prices and, babbling like a machine gun, assault head-on those people who, to begin with, are no experts, and who flee happy to have left no more than their purses behind.

The most disconcerting ingeniousness is to be found there. Everything, of course, is antique, very old, or prehistoric. The porcelains retail under a variety of labels, old Vienna, old Meissen, old Saxony, old Venice. A paraffin lamp would be called a candelabrum from Kutahya: "Anticas!"[1] A pot from Porrentruy would make a truly authentic base for a Mycenaean amphora—on condition, however, that handles and necks be bruised and bellies broken along the route.[2] The infatuation is especially with Persia. It seems that the gentlemen of the Bazaar have the same weaknesses I do. This is why they offered me, as if it came from Isfahan, one of those saucers, manufactured by the thousands for two or three years now at Villeroy and Boch in Germany—a crude hand-painted crockery, not at all bad-looking, and which sells for twenty-five pfenning per cup and saucer. This wise guy wanted twenty francs for it!

Another ingeniousness: in the window of a Turkish vendor there are small Persian lacquers, not very good, and also a tin-plated "Murattis" cigarette box; you know the kind, blue and red with gold threads. Nothing else was needed for one to hear:

—Oui, Moussu, Perse, antica. Moussu, Moussu!

I could tell you about many more of these ingenuities. I do not exaggerate!

Here in effect is Sesame, because one discovers and dislodges from beneath the piles of coarse earth the most sumptuous nuggets of the East, from the Islam of Europe to as far as the jungles, brought here piece by piece across the sands, mountains, and brush by the solemn caravans.[3]

It is a labyrinth (Baedeker recommends that one carry a compass), a maze of arcades, without a glimpse of sky for several kilometers. It is closed in, suffocating, and secluded. Here and there tiny windows pierce the low barrel vault, and yet it is well lit. It is deserted at night and frenzied during the day. At sunset, the heavy doors are drawn, enclosing the fabulous wealth, and the great clamor subsides.

Upon arriving, forewarned by the cries of these strange people, I could always imagine a metal god seated on the lintel of the door, rubbing his fat gold belly with both hands. His lips would be greedy, and his forehead would recede like that of an orangutan. His nostrils would be flared, and his gaze restless. He would have long donkey's ears. The hierophant sits there and in his slimy manner overhears the glib and deafening voices; he has the same features as his master, and as for his claws he has stolen them from the oldest of the bridges' tolltakers who died of grief. He speaks all languages badly, is dressed like us, and his hair is fuzzy. He is called Boorishness.[4]

Upon the two pillars of the portal where this god is enthroned are written the three commandments: "Thou shalt steal and lie!"—"Thou shalt lie in order to steal!"—"Steal, steal, steal!"

In the middle of the uproar I found myself being pushed into the central avenue. To the right and left streamed the shops, like chapels with squalid hardware and hideous carpets. Yet, for all that, there were many beautiful and fascinating things. You know that we admire with different eyes what we can buy for ourselves as opposed to what we see in the museums, where a feeling of melancholy frequently prevails because these things stagnate there, cold evidence rather than daily companions.

One does not enter a shop, one is sucked and shoved in; once inside the great machine, the "hustle" begins. The verbiage is insane, shouted by five or six who have almost dismembered you alive. There are several others who scream dreadfully. Of course they know what you want even before you do. The walls give way, the floor rises, the unfurled fabrics in their fast shuffle hurt your eyes. The merchants stuff them into your hands to feel, and under your nose to inspect the workmanship. There are embroideries as wide as table cloths from Bukhara; large, heavy, dark wool carpets from Izmir, Ankara, and Persia—then gauzes from Ioanina woven with silk and silver threads, the heavy Macedonian fabrics, the festive brocades, the textured velvets from Scutari, the block prints from Persia and India. Everything, the extraordinary with the trash, is brought out, spread, fluttered, whipped in your face, and piled up, helter-skelter.

The vampires have already understood your sign of refusal.

—So, it's not fabrics you want. I understand your taste. Here, there, here you are again!

Ceramics pile up, cluttering the glass tops of horizontal showcases that contain gilded brass jewelry and ivories of bone; antique earthenware from Kutahya, Persian tiles at fabulous prices stripped from some ruined mosque over there; two blue potbellied vases streaked with cracks, in which foods used to be preserved in oil, still greasy and stinking from their forgotten function. In the meantime, a broken Albanian shotgun or a Damascene dagger may be shoved in your face, so beautiful that the merchant has clicked his tongue! You will be forced to examine copper-engraved tinware that you did not want to see, and, since you may have mentioned lacquerware, here they are, ah yes, filling both your hands as they search in some closet for Korans whose pages they will flip through feverishly from end to end. When an illustration is astonishing in its archaic technique, conventional but imposing in style, they will cry:

—Monsieur, see how natural it is (for today's public—they know—prefers it to be like a photograph, with all the buttons or every leaf visible, as vivid as in the movies).

—Monsieur, it looks like it's going to speak. Monsieur! Monsieur! (They are always afraid that you are listening with only one ear.)

—Monsieur, it is antique! Then the climax of pleonasm.

—Monsieur, this manuscript, it is all handwritten, upon my word of honor.

Meanwhile carpets are not retrieved from their fall, nor embroideries from their swoon, nor pottery, now rendering every movement perilous. You are utterly seduced by a young Persian girl dressed in scarlet, beneath a golden canopy in an Isfahan garden with tulips and hyacinths everywhere. But they are still there, these horrible disciples of Boorishness, breathlessly scrutinizing the dark congested walls, eyes popping out of their heads to find the gadget that will ruin you. Truly, you cannot be cold-blooded any longer: there are too many crazy things before your eyes, too many delightful evocations that throw you into a foolish stupor. You are intoxicated; you cannot react at all. This torrent, this flood, this avalanche of charlatanism brutalizes and annihilates you.

They've got you at last! You didn't want to buy anything; you entered the place with a smile.[4] But you have dared to look too long at that *Bukhara*. You have been tempted. You are lost!

You said:

—How much? Hmm, hmm, euh, euheuh-euheuh. Euh! Hmm!

—Four hundred francs, Monsieur!

And you again said,

—Hmm!

But your hesitant "hmm" was another mistake. Now they are about to play a delightful comedy. From now on, just one will speak French; the others will play the role of the goggle-eyed Turk. But the gentleman speaking French is an open floodgate: it pours out!

—Yes, sir, four hundred francs, it is a gift, upon my word of honor! And to you alone, because you are my friend. (Just four hours ago, you were still looking for a room in Pera.) Because you are my friend, and I see you are a connoisseur; there are so many imbeciles who come here! (Here I am, little by little, very proud of myself.) And I want to have the honor to sell to a connoisseur! I want to strike a bargain with you from the beginning, so that you will come back, because you will be pleased! I want to strike a bargain with you— because it's Saturday, to finish the week!—because it's Sunday—I have this whim that I want to make a deal on Sunday, because it will bring me luck, so I am giving you an enormous discount; I am selling at a loss!

—Because it is Monday—to begin the week.—because it is Wednesday, and—just between us—it is a dead season, we don't sell a thing, look at my books. (He shows you a ledger with blank pages.)

—Ah, Monsieur, the cholera! It is Wednesday and I haven't sold anything yet! Monsieur, Monsieur! See this fabric. (It is shoved right against your eyes.) Feel this silk (you have handfuls of it)—this weight! Monsieur! (Whereupon, in a cloud of rising dust, they shove an entire bundle into your arms.) Then:

—Monsieur, upon my life! Upon my honor! Upon my conscience! Go around the whole Bazaar; and, if you find one piece like this one, I will give it to you and the money with it! I lose on it! Take it! (And here, he is whispering in your ear.) I told you four hundred francs; my brothers—those are my brothers there—my brothers don't know it. They don't understand French. They will be furious. God only knows what will happen to me, ah, I am going to be insulted! Then heroically:

—So much the worse, Monsieur, there are days when one is too hungry!

You walk out an hour later with the bundle under your arm. You have paid one hundred and fifty francs. And you are filled with remorse. For as soon as the shining money emerged from your purse, you saw their eyes glow. They were unable to play the comedy to the end, the sons of Boorishness. When they saw the gold they jumped at it like wolves.

Concerning this subject, Auguste remarked gravely:

—I believe these characters dream of the same hunger as our bedbugs, during our absence from Broussa, but for gold!

This is one corner of the Bazaar, a Greek corner. The Turk was driven out of here. After that he became corrupt. Actually he was decent, and he knew what he was selling.

# TWO FANTASIES, ONE REALITY

It is amid a western crowd, delirious with patriotic enthusiasm this Sunday evening in Naples where thirty thousand soldiers are embarking for Tripoli, that these recollections came surging back to me from an untimely lapse of memory.

We do not expect anything from that perfect twilight, when the air, its molecules gorged with light, turns the darkness of the night gray and opaque; the stars twinkle like crickets, and the moon lingers. Meanwhile the boat scuds along toward Stamboul whipped by the frosty air of the Bosphorus. We are returning from the burial ground at Scutari, where we have bruised our feet in the thistles of fields planted thick with tombstones. We have attended a fiery religious service by whirling Dervishes, of which I will say nothing just now because otherwise I would never finish.

The boat is off-shore from the dreadful palace of Dolmabahce.[1] Young Turkey, what a beginning! But what is this? Across the hill of Stamboul there are diamond necklaces suspended in the sky. Above one can glimpse an alabaster pinnacle, and below a long white shaft, watercolored in the haziness of the hour. As we enter the Golden Horn, the weather is fair; we escape from the approach of a sharp wind blowing across the channel, and coming from the steppes where wolves and fair-haired Cimmerians live.

The weather is mild, and there is a Turkish calm. This is the last boat, and facing the savage cleft of a black Pera riddled with lights, there are necklaces around the slender alabaster necks all along the crest of Stamboul. At dusk, they gleam like the round halos of oil lamps suspended beneath the domes of the mosques. They are of gold and have four tiers of fire. While we walk, the night becomes black and clear. Gold and black, supreme elegance, supreme power! And such serenity! One sees absolutely nothing, and not a sound can be heard. What is it then? The Turks are celebrating. One can feel that at this moment the mosques are humming with prayers and with stories exchanged between squatting old Turks in ample gowns, sometimes pink but usually black, and green turbans in the midst of white turbans.

I have understood. Over at the far right are six sets of three super-imposed necklaces, because this is the great Mosque of Ahmet. And at this majestic quadrangle, Pegasus descended from heaven, is Hagia Sophia, these four units at an immense distance. Nuruosmaniye obscures Bayazit. Then comes to view the sphinx which is Suleyman, above that its four minarets. Before long all is blurred because of the perspective. I recognize vaguely Shehzade, Sultan Mehmet, and Sultan Selim. And then straight ahead before the bridge, the minarets of Valide also glittering.

High above the New Bridge between Pera and Stamboul, at four o'clock in the morning, torn, disheveled, whitish patches of fog float across a background of opaque grey. Perhaps there is water in the Golden Horn, but no one can see it. Thick gauzes of mist whiten, tear, become white as snow. Then, heavy snowflakes fall, round and massive. They crush down, they submerge, they hide everything. Such dense fog, at four o'clock in the morning, is more obscuring than night itself. The dishevelment resumes; high up the nebulosity is accentuated by the fan-shaped unfolding of clear and dark streaks. Powerful vapors rise and come to life.

I am standing at the very edge of a half-raised pontoon bridge without a rail; it almost makes me dizzy. I hear shouts from below and then see rigs, slanted masts, large dark sails flapping and passing by. Through a break in the fog I see two flotillas on the right and the left, spreading their sails and hastening toward this channel between the open plat-forms. There are collisions, aborted maneuvers, boastful screams, and

*A flotilla of sailing boats on the Sea of Marmara (courtesy FLC). One of thirteen watercolors exhibited under the title "Langage de Pierre" in Munich (1911), Neuchâtel (1912), Zurich (1913), and Paris (at the Salon d'Automne, 1913)*

startling gestures. And all the while these masts, lines, and sails slip by and disappear into the opaqueness, now lit by the sun. Now that everything is brightened by the sun, the mist seems to become more opaque. It goes on tearing these disheveled clouds, it bores deep holes and scores victories. Vehemently the clouds return in hoards from behind the Golden Horn, where they must have been clinging to the cypresses in the cemeteries. All of a sudden I saw at the end of the bridge the Mosque of Validé, completely black. Then it disappeared. I looked up as the dark sphinx of Suleyman[a] was fading away. Afterward the entire forest of masts on the left was reddened by the sun and then drowned in a spray of water. The sun was gaining; the battle intensified; the clouds were losing control. At moments all the boats seemed to emerge from the Marmara, a misty plain of water. The exquisite triangles of vibrating sails looked like a harmony of tints. In the channel the boats hurried by. There is often only one man for each of these skiffs as large as those in the *Iliad*; barefoot, he holds the rudder with his stiffened legs; with his hands he pulls on the ropes. He jumps suddenly grasping the vast flapping sail when the wind takes it the wrong way. Then he grasps an enormous pole and, pushing against the other boats, shoves with all his might. Those were for us the most extraordinary gestures.

Steadily the clouds pressed on. There was no end to them. They rolled along with the boats, making the background appear sinister. The sun was worn out. Validé appeared still black, and nothing could be seen of Pera. In the meantime, high above the sky was turning pink. As

a. Suleyman and the Ahmet Cami are the biggest mosques in Stamboul. Cami means mosque. Often a mosque is named in memory of a sultan or pasha who built it. (Editor's note: This footnote dates from 1911.)

hundreds of boats were passing by, I saw this unforgettable sight: Suleyman, a delicate pink emerging from the dark draperies. For an instant it was deep blue against the pink clouds, but immediately after it turned alabaster white cold as granite. It kept appearing and reappearing, while the entire atmosphere sparkled with pink. The sea was asserting itself. Colors were appearing, but still very pale. In the distance boats could be seen bounding into that joy. The drama hastened on; the spectators increased in number. Valide took up its fixed position, and the exquisite Rustem Pasha came into view, harmonious in style and very small.[2] I have never seen Suleyman look so high; one could have thought it to be on a mountain and to have grown senselessly tall in a single night.

I turned around. In a chalky blue and frothy coral whirl was the Genoese Tower—a fantastic sight. It leans and rests upon a shoulder of tall houses spiked with chimney stacks. It is cylindrical, without a single window, and is capped by a projecting crown, closed, obtuse, and hard like a piece of machinery. The whole gigantic and somber apparatus looked like a tragic battleship. I thought I heard the wail of a siren, and I had a presentiment of something ominous, for I was a little beside myself.

A large pink cloud swept the apparition away. It returned and once more disappeared. Finally, the red disk of the sun asserted itself. It hurled terrible darts, it pierced the clouds, it triumphed. The mosques blanched, and Stamboul appeared, while the Genoese Tower straddled Pera, unyielding, red at the tip of its shoulder in shadow.

When the last vaporous layers were lifted, I thought I had been dreaming. The sails were disappearing, and a steamer had arrived from Scutari. The bridge had come down again, and, like a torrent, those

*The magnificent sphinxlike Mosque of Suleyman (courtesy FLC)*

from Stamboul, vegetable market gardeners, and hamals rushed for-
ward.³ The donkeys advanced gallantly, with tomatoes wrapped in vine
leaves. The porters, already dripping with sweat, were being crushed
beneath their incredible burdens. With their thin, worn legs trembling
within the thousand pleats of their funny trousers, they were swal-
lowed up by the funnel of Galata, at the point where a street steps
up toward the tower.
That was a reality—and inescapable! We left. We left a conquered and
adored city. We had been granted a twenty-four hour respite, which
meant that we had to undergo a "Young Turk" quarantine at the
mouth of the Black Sea. It was upon a large Russian liner packed with
black pilgrims, with Jews fleeing persecution, with Persians, with people
from the Caucasus dressed as though they were on stage (but much
better).
We had to pass Constantinople again. It was the middle of a sparkling
afternoon. As the ship's wake was rapidly opening to touch the green
banks of the Bosphorus, our hearts filled with melancholy at the sight
of the wooden konaks disappearing into the water. Sails were playing
with the wind ahead of us and became the harbingers of the apparition
that led us to the point where Asia, in an unforgettable spectacle,
abruptly withdraws from Europe. The light was behind Stamboul, giving
it a monolithic appearance. The shimmering light cast a plinth of
whiteness on the surface of the water where those sails passed and
where the silent steamers were fixed at anchor. Beyond the prow the
rooftops of the Seraglio rose in tiers between the cypresses and the
sycamores—a palace of poetry, a creation so exquisite that it cannot
be dreamed of twice. From there came the theory you already know.
The mist of light upon the sea was dissolving into this great back

*The Seraglio on a promon-*
*tory enclosed by a great*
*wall (courtesy FLC)*

*The Seraglio, Hagia
Sophia, and Ahmet, seen
from the sea (courtesy
FLC)*

lighting that extended as far as Mihrimah outlined against a sky annihilated with brightness. I don't believe I shall ever again see such *Unity*!

We passed by rapidly, I only wanted to look into the glaucous sea, where the boat's shadow marks immeasurable depths. For me it was as if the veil of my little temple had also been torn away!

# THE STAMBOUL DISASTER

The nightmare is over. What a tragic night! An awesome spectacle of fire, of impassive crowds, of upset crowds, of cries, and of tears. Elsewhere there was a celebration with brass bands, mean Chinese lanterns, idiotic firecrackers. I look through the window: at nine o'clock Stamboul, peaceful in the distance, is unchanged in the white morning light. As always the mosques from Suleyman to Ahmet pierce the blue sky. There is nothing strange. Yet 9,000 houses are now in ashes.

Yesterday we were on the opposite shore from Stamboul, between Pera and the Sweet Waters of Europe, upon a large plateau where grass does not stand a chance. It was Constitution Day; a crowd of Young Turks were at the parade. In the swirling opacity of the red dust, it was like the dreams of Raffet expressed in "Hodlerian" cadences: similar to those in the Jena mural where the dense ranks of armed students march endlessly.[1]

The army had paraded; then quite unexpectedly came the firefighters, all here by the hundreds. We were stupefied: What were these people doing here on such a day? For in this land, known for its unexpected attacks and its conspiracies, it was indeed the most propitious hour for carrying on reactionary vengeance. Only the day before we had wandered beyond the aqueduct, through an immense, deserted field that was the result of political vengeance two years ago in Stamboul. So today the firemen of Constantinople are on parade, while several hours away Stamboul is burning surreptitiously in three different places. Tired from the morning review, we were reading behind our closed shutters. By chance we put our noses to the window. Stamboul is crowned with a great black smoke, and flames are shooting out from the military headquarters. In the streets, groups of barefoot "volunteer firemen" are running about like raving madmen.

Having dressed, we rapidly go down through the Little Fields of the Dead, cross Galata, and arrive at the Golden Horn over the pontoon bridge. Stamboul rises in tier upon close tier of endless wooden houses submerged in greenery. Only the white blots of the mosques and a few administrative buildings brighten this carpet of violet and dark green. The crowd kept cramming onto the bridge, pushing toward the fire. One could already predict the enormous disaster.

We climb up the tortuous streets all lined with shops, near the Bazaar. A torrent of water, black with soot, runs down the street, followed by a torrent of hamals (street porters) and small artisans who without a word of complaint call out to clear the way for moving their furniture and tools. The inquisitive crowd keeps clambering up, and the police are not yet organized. Here we are at an obstructed street; the fire is burning houses on both sides, consuming the carpenters' district. In all the neighboring streets the shops are already emptied, the merchandise far away, under cover in some shed or in some mosque transformed into a furniture warehouse. The proprietors are sitting and smoking with friends, watching for the arrival of the flames, ready to clear out.

Three places caught fire simultaneously; at first it was the government buildings around the Ministry of Defense. Then the district adjacent to the Yeni Validé Mosque.[2] Completing the triangle: those real Turkish streets near the Mosque of Shehzade, with the wooden dwellings of thousands of small artisans. The immense triangle had to close, and, with the wind pressing upon the blaze during the night, it was to form a trapezoid encompassing two million square meters, as far as Sultan Mehmed on one side and the sea at Veni Capon on the other![3]

By nightfall we are in the Sultan Bayazit Square. The three infernos had joined, and the wind changes and threatens the Bazaar. It would

A *Stamboul street scene,*
*"tier upon close tier of*
*endless wooden houses*
*submerged in greenery"*
*(courtesy FLC)*

be a dreadful ruin. One by one the shopkeepers arrive; the shops light up, and the merchandise accumulates in front of the doors. Throngs of hamals escorted by mounted police come and carry everything away. Carriages go by, overloaded, drawn by impassive oxen or horses that rear up in fear. One often risks getting run over.

The blaze advances, spreading into streets from both ends, and the houses empty one by one. The small artisans continue to move out: one, here, bent double under the load of an enormous mirror, three over there straining to carry a cupboard filled with linen. Another, a carpenter, carries his workbench while his sons follow with planks. Veiled women escape slowly, crying, and pulling squalling youngsters. From a house threatened by the flames, a corpse is carried away, already shut in its coffin; six stooping men run, taking it away into the crowd. Where will they deposit this strange package?

The crowd blocks the streets, unperturbed and curious. It hinders these poor people plagued by the fire who would like to rescue their belongings, and neither a gesture of compassion nor one of solidarity induces this multitude of idlers to offer assistance. All these Turks in long silk gowns and white turbans look on gravely; the cafés overflow into squares, and the trees barely protect the people from the downpour of burning embers flying frenetically in the sky. The street vendors sell their lemonade, their syrups, their ice-cream, their fruit. It seems like an intermission at a theater where a great, extraordinary spectacle is performed, but whose audience is blasé because they know it all and nothing more can interest them. For Stamboul has been burning like this for centuries.

At the horizon, the sky is getting dark and changes from emerald green to a deep ultramarine diluted with green like a glaucous sea.

Against it, the minarets and domes of Bayazit are outlined in a splendid unity, incomparably majestic, carved out of solid gold. At times, one can see in the blazing panorama and beneath the immense cloud of golden smoke, other minarets as white as overheated iron. Whirlwinds of glowing embers, dancing diabolically, fly off to carry the devastation hundreds of meters away. Since we do not see a convulsive face, we have no sense of horror. We hear no groans, no cries, no blasphemies other than the curses of overburdened hamals, and no fists are raised toward the sky. We are captivated by a scene of formidable beauty, and haunted by its magnificence. We are drawn by these golden columns like those houses that get absorbed by the fire, and now we can only seek to appease this passion that overwhelms us by its diabolical beauty. We seek the beautiful spectacles. We discuss the fantasy created by domes and minarets. We find at last the part of Constantinople of grandeur and magic we had dreamed of. A breath of imperial Byzantine madness is mixed up with a fatalistic and cynical sensuality. If one goes from one viewpoint to another, it's to get a better view of the contrast between the black disc of a dome outlined against a brocade of fire and the solemnity of an obelisk. We circle the colossal blazing mass as though it were a sculpture; we stand before the joyous shower of sparks, searching for a favorable viewpoint as if in front of a painting. An astronomer would find fantastic and novel Milky Ways in these fabulous columns of smoke, streaming with fiery embers. It is an exaltation of joy! What utter joy!

Slowly we go down again toward the Golden Horn, having admired from the bridge the marvelous spectacle of immense mosques, awesome in purple and gold and a hundred times larger than we knew them to be by daylight, a little fantastic, a little mad.

We went up again to the Little Fields of the Dead where in the solitude of brown sand, the last gravestones are coming loose. From the terrace of our house, the spectacle becomes coherent. This time the Golden Horn is on fire (the ugly one, always so apathetic!); it streams down like molten steel and appears to carry the black, untouched bar of Stamboul. Upon the crest of the mountain, where by day one can see the infinite display of the sea of Marmara and the mountains of Asia across the tops of the houses, the flame of this colossal sacrifice now rages. The black and sharp minarets of the Suleyman and Shehzade mosques like giant skewers pierce this flesh of fire. The mosques of Bayazit to the left and Mehmet to the right receive its warm caress and turn to alabaster. Their white and mystical minarets disappear in the sky above. They mark the two edges of that unforgettable altar. Yet they are separated by more than two thousand meters. The aqueduct of Valens seems to want to unite them, and out of the innumerable openings of its arches, flames are leaping out as from the portholes of a blazing ship.

It is one o'clock in the morning. The wind blows the flames even farther. The fantastic plume of the fire swells to full size and then begins to subside. There we stand before this spectacle that is beyond understanding and leaves us stupid, overcome by a great melancholy. Looking anguished at the thrashings of this enraged dragon, we repeat over and over: It's horrible, it's horrible![4]

*The Aqueduct of Valens*
*(courtesy FLC)*

It's over, and yet I haven't said a thing! Not even a word about Turkish life—a word! It would take a book. Our meager seven weeks did not suffice to give us a glance of it. For this reason, I've held my tongue on this subject. Believe me, for each of my sentences a hundred more are missing. To speak of Stamboul and not to describe its life is to remove the soul from those things I have spoken of. Had I done it by telling you of the harmony between *that* life and *its* milieu, I would have had the opportunity to speak to you about the hideous disaster, the catastrophe that will inevitably ruin Stamboul: the advent of modern times. In that year I saw the twilight of Constantinople.

Here then are some scattered notes to retrieve from oblivion a few recollections of the past, and a few regrets as well.

A Catholic sanctuary, no longer alive for us, inhabited by spirits, according to some dreamy vagabonds, dark and gloomy with its old paintings, presents to the rare visitor some faded iconostasis, with a Christ on the Cross, the Transfiguration, the Apparition, and in the center an angel in a blazing sky announcing to a trembling Virgin redemption for centuries to come. Such is the paradise of the Diocesan Archbishop in Bucharest.[1] Sometimes I have quoted the remarks of my august companion, and yet I have never described him. Here is his portrait.

Ancestry: Flemish but crazy about modern Paris. His people tighten the lips on the letter "b," which they obliterate. As to his personality: a decent fellow. And here are a few small revealing details about him. He dares to love Jordaens, Brouwer, and Van Ostäde, about whom he says,

—Long may they live! They drink, laugh, eat![2]

At those times when we were in agonizing misery, reduced literally to nothing but black bread, he would disappear furtively behind street corners to buy cigars. He nearly died when all we could fill our drinking glasses and coffee cups with was water!

Another revelation of his real self (once when we spent the night on a bench): he awakes, sits up, rolls eyes heavy with sleep which he fixes on me in a long gaze, and after a seeming eternity, and while regaining consciousness, he wonders out loud:

—*Maype we could have* a *peer!* (as if there were a keg right there under the bench!)

Another revealing event in Pera (this time Auguste has all the bedbugs in his bed): at three in the morning he lights the candle and starts roasting them. He gets all excited in pursuit of these mean little vermin who burrow under his long fingernails (because he has style, this art historian, this theoretician!). He taps his fingernails on the marble table top, and the tiny beasts drop out; he runs them through with his writing pen, then fries them; the cadavers drown in the hot wax, next day forming a nougat, conspicuously Turkish. Auguste perspires, and once the massacre is accomplished, he cannot help but conclude:

—Oh, la, la, let's roll a little cigarette!

He goes back to sleep, the pacifier in his mouth, happy about the carnage, and complacent with his smoke!

Another thing: he is an absolute Gascon, he has an imagination which he expresses through grand gestures and exaggerations.[3] He led one of Papa Bonnal's nephews, who had never been anywhere but Cairo, to believe that in our country the winter brings us twenty meters of snow.

Twenty! The nephew nearly caught a cold in amazement! And then:

—Oh, yes, one day in Florence—by the way the Florentines never take a bath!—this confirmed one day in Florence, when I went swimming under the Ponte Vecchio. A huge crowd was leaning against the parapet to watch me. So, to startle them, I, all naked in the middle of the river, calmly lit a cigarette!

Auguste, physically: the build of a fakir.

After spending a whole day looking for a room in Pera, he stared at the last signs saying "furnished rooms" with the wide-open look of a fish in a basket.

He eats with the conviction of a sleeping cat and the seriousness of a drinking cow! Jordaens, Brouwer! Auguste, when I send these articles to the editor of this little journal, I will beg him to omit this defamatory information!

His Holiness Ghénadié, the former Diocesan Archbishop of Hungaro-Walachia, in a way the Pope of these regions, did not offer a prayer before the meal, when he received us. He sought to welcome us only in the most cheerful way possible so he spoke of art and of the political and social economy. He had the head of a superb "Rubenesque" Pan, and his table was covered with lilies. That day we were chauffeured around Bucharest from monastery to monastery in the car of the Secretary of the Interior. All days are not alike!

Philosophy from Bucharest, one evening after dinner. Auguste and I agree: Protestantism as a religion lacks the necessary sensuality that fills the innermost depths of a human being, sanctuaries of which he is hardly conscious and which are a part of the animal self, or perhaps the most elevated part of the subconscious. This sensuality, which intoxicates and eludes reason, is a source of latent joy and a harness of living strength. Ronsard, who embraced Catholicism because he found in it this fundamental principle, said that if he were ever to give it up, it could only be to become a pagan; he would then join the savages, "who happily follow the law of nature." For we are among those bruised by the dreadful austerity of our rigid and narrow-minded morals.

Whenever in Pera I watch an orthodox funeral procession go by with its uncovered corpse, livid and disgusting in the light of the sun and swarming with flies, it shocks and repulses me. Why this parade of *horror?* Is the intention to make everyone who encounters it reflect on the inevitability of death? Shouldn't it rather exhort us to the good life? To live well and harmoniously and to enjoy our earthly blessing should be, I believe, our aim. The rest does not concern us. When death comes, we all have to surrender, because she is so much the stronger. But, before it is over, at least we should have something, and let us look good at the departure!

Now I am either about to contradict myself or to make myself clearer: peasant art procedes from the art of the city. It belongs to it as one of its by-products. It is a cross-breed, but still beautiful, with interesting characteristics and, in any case, showing powerful strength. Primitive art is a precursor. Fortunately the peasant remains a real primitive man when he creates. Still he has his bad taste, his pride, and his laziness. That is why he steals from the city its style and its language, but he will reinterpret them unconsciously and with naiveté! It is an innate strength that bursts out in spite of and almost against itself. This is very strange, but it brings about art works full of awkwardness and barbarism which appeal to our sophisticated tastes. Look at the peasant houses on the Rumanian plain: they have a dazzling and astounding brilliance; the stucco is white, the base an intense blue; the corners are painted or shaped, representing pilasters; the pillars that border the windows and pediments are painted a strong blue, sometimes set off by a glorious yellow. These are classical architectural elements, but they are all used incorrectly because there is no base under the columns and no entablature above them. The capital (the flower, the *ornament*) is its aim, and an end in itself. Because, even if the *vocabulary* has been that of the city (because of a pathological inclination toward "bourgeoisism"), the soul, the aspirations, and the hand are those of a primitive man. It is painted with gusto on a spring day, to last a whole year and to provide the peasant with a festive setting and a gay and colorful shelter. *He wants to feel decent and like a king in his palace.* Thus the primitive man wraps himself in bright colors and creates beauty all around him.

This means that the city should not return to the country; it would be as though one were to give to the symptoms the disease itself as a cure. The city must follow its own course and be reborn on its own. It owes it to itself, and besides, it cannot do otherwise.

As to landaus and other large carriages with springs used in the Balkans: after two hours of bumping along in the only cart from the village of Shipka, we arrived at Kazanlŭk. All our teeth had fallen out; we felt as if we had a mouthful of them. And just as we were considering addressing our grievances to the driver, here he goes, finding four holes we (or rather our backsides) had made in the seatboard. So, very respectfully, we shook hands with the good fellow and gave him a few sous with which to buy springs—please! Auguste recalled with horror his tooth pulled by a barber in Tŭrnovo, whereas this time, it had been accomplished painlessly. For a lot of people, common folk as well as high society, a painter at work in the streets is something of a public attraction like a kiosk, a newsstand, or a barometric column.

Everyone comes to watch him. So he has to undergo the very distressing and tactless presence of a crowd of simpletons who will not even spare him their reflections. He should in fact be delighted, if at least they would refrain from planting themselves between himself and his subject!

The traveler's friends: They must be sent postcards and letters. As you were leaving they cried out to remind you that "you must bring back pictures and souvenirs!" You sweat a lot, and you even have to fight to conquer the coveted objects. Your friends let you down. They even envy you. You never receive an answer from them. It seems that they ignore your address which often changes. So their letter may well be lost, or arrive too late or too early!—Oh, those very dear, very busy friends!

Some cheerful quotes from Baedeker.[a] In a museum of mosaics: "On the wall to the right, parrots, a wild cat with a partridge, and on the middle pillar below the mosaic, fish. An assembly of seven philosophers . . ."

Concerning Pentelicus, the mountain from which came the radiant marble of the Acropolis: "The summit equipped with a trigonometric sign was adorned in antiquity by a statue of Athena."

Finally in the section on Constantinople, something like this: "There, where the railroad warehouses are today, once stood the temple of Venus . . ."

There was the Stone Age, the Bronze Age, the Iron Age, and then the Age of Pericles. But nowadays, two thousand three hundred years later, comes the age of oil cans, spreading all over eastern Europe,

a. Baedeker is a traveler's guide printed in different languages which is similar to the Joanne guides.

marking a new state of civilization and applied arts. In the East until now they used red earthen jars with a purely classical profile. A few women still return from the wells in the posture of the biblical Esther, but they are rare, and in this age, ten-liter tin cans equipped with wooden handles deal a death blow to the ceramic arts. Tin is less brittle. People don't pause for poetic daydreams in the twilight of an oasis!

Well then, in two thousand years under three meters of humus and debris, countless discoveries will be made; and instead of archaic terra-cotta the esteemed brand of Batum petroleum will turn up.[4] One day under the Hippodrome everything will be unearthed, from glassware and gilded shells from Germany to gramophone records. On the other hand, who is to say that someone inspired by the excavations of the House of the Golden Cupids at Pompeii won't uncover Turkish stools made in Venice from between the walls of our house in northern Europe or that the lavas of Pouillerel won't leave intact within an artificial stone stair shaft a well-polished little negro boy holding up the lantern of "good taste."[b]

Turkish aphorisms: Where there are no houses, there are tombs. Thus the land is always inhabited. Their country is a desert; wherever they build, they plant trees. Compared to the East, our country is a paradise; wherever we build, we chop down the trees. Stamboul is an orchard, and La Chaux-de-Fonds, a field of stone.

b. The artificial stone is a form of concrete, beginning to appear on building sites. Pouillerel is a rounded hill rich in Jurassic stone which is basically not volcanic. The well-polished little negro boy is a piece of sculpture at the head of a stair carrying a mass-produced lantern of Venetian origin, which was brought home from a honeymoon in the land of the Doges.

The Young Turkey at the Sweet Waters of Europe: some Turks in a caïque brought along their phonograph and let themselves be lulled by the murmur of the waves and the shrill sound of the awful megaphone.[5] The bourgeoisie of Paris are unaware of such refinement in their small suburban boxes. In a café beneath the plane trees a jolly old fellow plays endlessly on the bagpipes; it is always the same refrain continuing for hours. In a certain way he embodies the deep perseverance of his people. Soon he'll die, and there will be no one to replace him: his Master's Voice has already crossed the threshold, victoriously.[6] Stamboul will die. The reason is that she is always burning and being rebuilt. The immense district around the aqueduct of Valens, which was ravaged a few years ago, has been rebuilt by a *Company* (weigh the significance of these words for Stamboul!), by a *German Company*. (After what I've tried to tell you about the streets of Stamboul, shaded by the foliage between the salmon-colored walls, you should tremble at the association of these two words!)

Just what do you suppose they wrote in the local papers about the disaster that I had previously described to you—guess, you really didn't read it! Such progress! I repeat myself: People don't pause to daydream *before* the twilight of an oasis! They move on!

The konak, the Turkish wooden house, is an architectural masterpiece. (On every page of his book Theophile Gautier wrote that it was a hen coop—proof that the dogmas of art are as immutable as those of the Holy Father!)

"The Cholera and the Crisis of *Carpous and Peponis*" is a thesis for an anemic social economist! The carpous is a round melon, dark green and completely smooth on the outside, madder-red with black seeds on the inside. The *peponi* is an oval melon, completely smooth and

Two types of konak, the
Turkish wooden house—
"an architectural master-
piece" (courtesy FLC)

golden yellow on the outside, golden red on the inside, and more flavorful than the carpous. Both give a first-rate diarrhea. The Turk digests them vigorously: he lives with his harem and his melons. At any rate I know that he overdoes it with the latter. Each morning at the Golden Horn I saw dozens of incoming boats yellow with peponis and green with carpous. One day, within twenty-four hours, a hundred Turks, Greeks, Armenians, and Maltese were stricken by a deadly epidemic of cholera that gave them tremors that could be picked up as far away as Greenland, so a firman prohibited the consumption of carpous and peponis![7] What came of it? I don't know, since we ran off to Athens!

On the seventeenth of August of this year the typographer at *La Feuille d'Avis* had linen at home to be washed; note that on the eighteenth, preoccupied with his household concerns, he wrote about the flower day in Vienna: "overflowing with colors and linen displays." It was supposed to be "luxurious displays." "Linen" scarcely corresponds to the spirit of Maria Theresa, Marie Antoinette, of those aristocratic ladies dallying along the tree-lined avenues of the Prater on a gay day in May!

I'll be serious again.

"How painful it is to meet tourists!" I wrote one day in my travel diary. They are philistines in exodus, noticed more than ever because they are outside their milieu and stand out. You see them, but especially you hear them because their footsteps are as confidant as their taste, and they stride along their art pilgrimages proclaiming oracles.

Never is their admiration for the artist's ideas. Paste and imitation gold thrills as intensely as ever. They are in ecstasy over the *work*. "What a job!," "It's the work of Romans," "It's all handmade!" About the materials they will say, "It's not painted, it's mosaics! My God, it must have cost a fortune!" As they depart: "Yes, that was really beautiful!"

Yet they are only truly moved when this bric-a-brac is gold-colored, ostentatious, indecent, and horribly displayed. The public doesn't know anything anymore; it has lost a sense of proportion. People are driven crazy by theories; so they don't know what to do to purge or to educate themselves. They too have caught that dreadful germ that is going to ruin innocent countries' hearts, hitherto simple and believing, and the arts that were until now normal, sane, and natural. What I have seen on the way takes away from me forever all faith in the ingeniousness of new races, and I place all my hopes in those who, having started from the beginning, are already well advanced and know much. That's why I believe there is no need to react. Purification is a vital necessity, and as we avoid death by the simple desire to live, we shall return—yes, to the health that belongs to this epoch, a health appropriate to our contingencies, and then from there to beauty. Throughout the world, we *are recovering;* the scales are falling from our eyes. The infectious germ will be opposed by a youthful, vigorous, joyous germ born of the need "to conquer or to die."[c]

No one wants to die.

Well, the confusion is complete, and the deviation from enthusiasm irreparable. I met in Bulgaria a Frenchman with his wife, returning from Constantinople, who said to me in an enraptured voice:

c. It took me sixty years to locate the crucial point from which the knowledge of and the taste for contemporary art has spread. It seems to be the invention of offset printing which advanced the direct and integrative use of photography, in other words, automatic utilization without hand assistance, a true revolution!

—Oh, yes, we had a good time, but what a pity the streets are so filthy.

His wife quickly corrected him:

—But no, that's precisely what I find so chic!

Both finally agreed that they were delighted with their two weeks spent there.

Since we were not at all well-informed, we asked a Bulgarian which city we should see, Philippolis or Adrianople.[8]

—Philippolis, gentlemen, it is modern, it has wide straight streets, it's clean! Adrianople is a filthy Turkish city!

We went to Adrianople, but we thought that something in his judgment was nevertheless worth retaining for the art of tomorrow.

A Greek dentist we met in Constantinople who had been practicing for many years in Cairo said:

—Ah, Cairo? It is a hundred times more beautiful than here! Oh, but certainly, because they *have the English over there!* By all means, go there. It's just like a European city. You'll love it there, you'll see lots of paved streets. And then there are the streetcars, and the hotels, fifty or a hundred times bigger than this one here. You must not fail to see Heliopolis; the houses there are brand new.[9]

Dumbfounded, I inquire about the Arab city, the white city with mouchorabies and polychrome minarets, and then about the museum in which everything of Egypt will soon be housed.[10]

—Yes, yes, I know all that, but after all it's not the real Cairo!

On the other hand, he knew about the Pyramids.

# RECOLLECTIONS OF ATHOS

An alarming eclecticism predisposes us daily to a doting tolerance, and we misestimate the present. What a hodgepodge of antiquated ideas occupies most of our intellectual pursuits. Our practical and effective actions are weak and uncertain because we have been petrified, like Lot's wife, for having looked too long behind us. Nevertheless, I feel a mortal sense of shame, a contempt for myself—aviators kill themselves trying to fly like birds, extravagant ocean liners, creations sprung from a mere century of engineering labor, are lost at sea for having tried to gain a few hours crossing an ocean; tunneled mountains no longer present an obstacle; and so it goes.

At the end of a intermixed Bach and Handel concert bursts forth Franck's "Finale for Organ!" Shouts, heavy breathing, blows, a gigantic push forward, the obstacle overcome, the dazzling light in the clamors and cries of heros who battle! One's whole being is conquered, reborn, and elevated, and pride rightfully takes its place on our brows.

Oh, this Athos unduly doomed to death, as if by a vow of self-destruction! And so imbued with deep-felt poetry! Yes, to go there requires physical courage not to doze off in the slow narcosis of so-called prayer but to embark, rather, upon the immense vocation of a trappist—the silence, the almost superhuman struggle within oneself, to be able to embrace death with an ancient smile!

---

That first evening, as we disembarked at the little port of Daphni, I thought we had landed on some island of long ago, since every vestige evoked a poetry shaped by an adoration for the past. The moment was not simply bucolic. It was also sacred, filled with silence and peace.

For three days at sea our souls were overcome with a kind of floating repose in which reverie takes flight, mingled with more compelling ideas of personal creation for the years to come—mere dreams, no, more like hopes.

Sensations, manifold and extreme, virile and languid. During the peaceful crossing under the sky of Islam, we pondered our actions, and reactions, undisturbed since we gave up our meals at the communal table. Encamped on the prow, we lived like gypsies, opening our eyes to the piercing greens of the dawn and overwhelmed by the midday heat. In the evening hours, seated on large coils of rope or the anchor, we watched the incomparable richness of the coming sunset simultaneously animated by the sky, its trophies sparkling in the sunlight; our flesh throbbed with resurging blood. Lying motionless late at night, I feigned sleep, so that I could gaze, with eyes wide open, at the stars and listen, with ears fully cocked, for every trace of life to subside, savoring *silence* in its glory. These were the happiest hours I have ever experienced, and overwhelming memories of them have been with me for three years now.

I think that the flatness of the horizon, particularly at noon when it imposes its uniformity on everything about it, provides for each one of us a measure of the most humanly possible perception of the absolute. In the radiant heat of the afternoon, suddenly there appears the pyramid of Athos! Like a solemn effigy, it stands erect for several hours until, in a rapid enlargement, with its two thousand meters rising above sea level, it towers over us. The pilgrims, poor devils, more tense than we are by the gradual approach of this sight, maintain among themselves a radiant and anxious silence, which gives this instant, when

The pyramid of Mount
Athos rising two thousand
meters above the sea
(courtesy FLC)

the propellers stop spinning after the orders from the bridge, the solemnity of a judgment. The grinding of chains, the submerged anchors, immobility.

The obsession for symbols that lies deep inside me is like a yearning for a language limited to only a few words. My vocation may be the reason for this: the organization of stone and timber, of volumes, of solids and voids, has given me, perhaps, a too general understanding of the vertical and the horizontal, and of the sense of length, depth, and height as well. And I think that such elements, and these very words, which possess infinite meaning, do not need to be clarified, since such a word, in its complete and powerful unity, expresses them all. To go even further, I imagine color in bands of yellows, reds, blues, violets, and greens, with sharp boundaries but otherwise like a rainbow of lines going from the vertical to the horizontal without the bisecting slope. Let rhythm alone arrange this pure graphic expression! I will let my training waste away, with its scruple for details instilled in me by my teacher. Beholding the Parthenon, its mass, columns, and architraves, will satisfy me as does the sea in itself—and nothing else but this word; the same way the Alps, the very symbol of height, of depth, and of disorder, or the cathedral will be sights important enough to require all my strength. Hence, to view any house with its multiple parts will evoke the same displeasure as stubbing a toe against a stone dropped from a rock crusher, and though I admire Claude Monet, I will be outraged by him and hail Matisse. To me, the entire Orient seemed to be molded into majestic symbols. I recall the vision of a yellow sky, even though it was often blue; that of brown earth, as well as the unique memory of stone temples, and wattle huts or wooden houses of men. This same frame of mind makes me think it crazy to seek a shape for a vase other than the millennial form produced all over the world. I would prefer geometric combinations, the square, the circle, and proportions in simple and distinctive ratios. Wouldn't it take me a lifetime of labor to harness these simple and eternal forces, fraught with the uncertainty of ever attaining the proportions, unity, and clarity worthy of even a little country cottage built in accordance with the invaluable laws of an age-old tradition?

So, in the dazzling evening that followed our arrival at Daphni, I immensely enjoyed the sharp uphill climb of our mules, connecting, in their steady progress, the enormous side of this mountain to the sea and to the ridge, beyond which the sea would reappear even more boundless than before. It was a magic conjuration of those primary elements—the sea and the mountain with its symbol dedicated to the Virgin—and the intoxicating embrace of the moist evening, wafting voluptuously from the mountainside in warm fragrances drawn from so many young trees, from so many universally symbolic species—mulberry, olive, fig, the vine, immense bramble, and unchanging hollies—and then, all the way up on a high mountain terrace, cypresses surprised us there; they seemed like twenty melancholic sentinels guarding this vast and extended cloister of Xiropotamou, and lording over the scene in the setting sun.[1] My mule slowed down. It was very late; night was falling. We had climbed so many steep and undulating slopes in a continuous ascending effort. A dry stone wall began to cut into the slope, then suddenly rose up into a huge rampart. At its base grew the cypresses, which dominated its gray mass from above. What an incredible sky! Then all the way up at the top of the wall was my first glimpse of monastic life: a young monk with an olive complexion, nobly framed by his black beard, greeted me from that height with a touching bow, his arms crossed on his chest. The mule trotted over and then drank for a long time from a fountain gushing out from the rampart. Suddenly, off again, with that youthful strength and fury common to mules, it carried me up the widely paved ramp to the courtyard where right before my eyes I saw the first of the monasteries.

We saw so many of them during those eighteen days that followed! But this sight remains the most moving, the most nobly benevolent. It was the porch of an ancient fortress, together with smooth bare walls, on top of which perched cellular dwellings high up in the sky with their galleries open to the sea.

Farther on, having turned and pulled my mule to a stop, I saw the monastery from above and discerned the delightful presence of lead-covered domes, reminders of Stamboul. A spacious horizontal plane terminated the quadrilateral of buildings and directed my attention far away to the faint sea. The cypresses were black, the monastery a delicate gray, the olive trees silver green, and the sky a harsh green with streaks of violet coming from the sea. Directly above, white stars entered onto that changing scene whose footlights were not being extinguished as the performance unfurled in black and gold, with the clattering hooves of the mules on the sandstone pavement of sleeping Karies.[2]

We went back down as many slopes as we had climbed, and houses came into view, situated among vines. A few kerosene lamps were burning inside street lanterns hanging here and there. A radiant silence gave us the feeling of truly arriving in a promised land. An open door at the end of the street projected a bright light onto the pavement, illuminating a wall of vines on which we saw hanging grapes. It was the inn, the main hall of which was sparsely decorated with all those fatuous posters that internationalize cafés today. Quickly crossed, it opened onto a wide wooden balcony, a true example of construction on piles, whose height that evening seemed to us very big. The vine branches over the ancient pergola, just like those above the wine-press of Benozzo Gozzoli in Pisa, and like the painted trellis over the house illuminated from below by the hanging lanterns, were rippling in the night air, displacing all sense of values and offering for our enjoyment a new and absolutely imperial impression, completely interwoven with these lavishly situated fantasies.[3]

The hill stretched down toward the sea, and from a high suspended terrace, to which we gained access by crossing a wide hall, we caught a glimpse of the sea, framed by the nervous architecture of a wooden trellis covered entirely with vines whose clusters of blue and golden grapes hung heavily down.

Within the natural nooks of leaves and tendrils stood some tables; others pressed against the railing, and if they deprived their guests of bacchanalian groves that would have delighted Silenus, they at least opened up to the eyes of Bacchus and his young followers, in a space more noble and filled entirely with the sky, the sea where fishing boats seldom pass, and the broad folds of earth as huge as those of a tempest, where grapes, mulberries, olives, and figs bulge, promising a rich harvest. The night was conducive to any emotional contemplation made languid by the warm, moist air, saturated with sea salt, honey, and fruit; it was also conducive, beneath the suspended, protective pergola, to the fulfillment of kisses, to wine-filled and amorous raptures.

It is rather strange that there isn't here a more resolute architecture, with some marble banisters, and that behind us, the wall of the palace isn't made of stucco, modulated with architectural fantasies revealing the simulated depths of atriums, and that the stairway does not climb some seraglio. This evening, my heart would also take pleasure in some Hesperides or Cytherea that Watteau may conceive for us. With the overwhelming heat of the evening and our sudden transplantation into the sensuous night of such a place, a more than Pompeii-like feeling resonates with a heavy languor, and the loneliness of my heart conjures, in this glowing warmth, the black outfit and dismal figure of a marquis standing away from the group, far from the tables beneath the lattices and vine-leaves, and leaning against the railing, back turned, lost in the contemplation of the sea.[4]

No, for over a thousand years, this very simple and unique inn in Karies has lodged neither a marquise nor a courtesan, not even a simple woman traveler. For this land with the most Dionysian of suns and the most elegiac of nights is dedicated only to the dejected, the poor, or the distressed, only to the noble souls of trappists, only to criminals fleeing the laws of men or sluggards fleeing work, only to dreamers and seekers of ecstasy and solitude.

The next day, high above the upper gallery where the stairway led us, we saw innumerable chapels surrounded by an abundance of vineyards, figs, mulberries, olives, and poplars, chapels of a timid Byzantine style, made of dry stones with quite shrunken, very small, lead-covered domes, with fortresslike walls, and drawbridges. We saw them stretching out across the hills, over the rocks, and over the beaches, alternately minuscule, immense, gay, tragic, graceful, austere and vicious, forthright, and furtive beneath a white sun, with the sky and the atmosphere filled with a radiant splendor rippling the glossy and boundless fields of the sea.

————

Lying crumpled along the roadsides of the city of Karies, filthy, crippled, dissolute monks, perhaps infected with leprosy, beg us to throw them alms. They arouse indignation because so much idleness, vice—who knows what else—show what had brought them there. What, on the other hand, if it were some lamentable bad luck endlessly pursuing them that had cast them up on the Holy Mountain as though in a safe harbor, and if they had found there only cruel selfishness and indifference to their woes? What if the vine branches, the fig trees, and mulberries, even the rye grown behind fences, had been denied them because they hadn't earned them? The large sandstone paving slabs in the four or five streets of Karies are hard on their sores, and what a bed for their weariness!

The Virgin has her altar on the great mountain consecrated entirely to her praise. Her altar has its monastery at the foot of the mountain, on a sandy bank by the edge of the sea. The monastery is a big quadrangle pierced by a door at the end of a former drawbridge; washed by the moat, the enclosing walls are bare almost all the way to the top, where balconies cling and where loggias open at the fourth and fifth floors. In the middle of the large courtyard is the main church, Byzantine to its roots, in its form and its eternal principles. A Byzantine spirit still pervades the whole of this monastery, even down to its smallest stones. But many other monasteries, eighteen I think, sit like eagles' eyries at the top of steep, inaccessible rocks.[5] Others, similar to this one, are near the sea. Everywhere there is an aura of another age and, because of the multitude of monks, a feeling of disturbing anachronism.

From Karies we go down to the monastery specially devoted to the

View of Simonos Petras,
one of the many monaster-
ies perched "like eagles'
eyries at the top of steep,
inaccessible rocks" of
Athos (courtesy Jean Petit)

Virgin Mary to attend her festival on the seashore at the foot of a tremendous pyramid crowned with white marble, Athos, the two thousand meter high mountain. By the time the sun reaches the side of the mountain this evening, the doors of the monastery of Iberians will close behind the pilgrims who have come from across the entire peninsula to intoxicate themselves with liturgical chants, or to eat, to eat—the poor, the dissolute, the wretched dying of hunger—because, during this annual festival the refectory, an enormous stone vault enlivened by an antique idol (at the heart of an imperious white apse), stays open all night.[6] But at night inside the main church, with its dark walls dimmed by countless, adjoining Byzantine frescoes, they will chant until morning, poignant, hallucinatory litanies.

Joy, celebration, the sun, and a nature covered with vines, fig trees, and poplars. Before us the sea indicates midafternoon through its pale refraction over all the green of this infinitely sloping terrain. We go down to the sea. Young hermits dressed in the blue smocks of working friars are seated in an enclosure at the entrance to a vineyard. Nearby is their skete, a tumulus of dry stones, the refuge of their double life.

—Hello! We call out to them with sudden cheer.

One of them rises quickly, runs into the vineyard and returns loaded down with a bunch of grapes, his spontaneous offering. Two of the hermits smile and bow, their hands crossed over their chests.

—Hello, friends. Thank you, thank you!

———————

The sea is a long way from this high-perched monastery. From our white rooms the horizontal view is endless; we have never seen the horizon from such latitude, nor in such a season. The blurring of heat interposes and merges the sea and the sky, and only rippling waves reveal to the watchful eye the tangible presence of a body of water. The view downward from our windows is dizzying; we are on the highest floor of the monastery, at the top of a sheer rocky cliff. The church courtyard, paved with gray stones, is a uniform oxblood color: all the way from the foundation up to the marvelous gray, lead-covered domes.

We entered the refectory escorted by the temporal prior of these working monks: a black and hairy crowd stands on each side of two long tables, linked at one end by the table of their superior, and forming a horseshoe shape in front of the apse sanctified by an icon of gold. We take the places reserved always for the expected guest. Today the pilgrim from Jerusalem doesn't join us at all, a man who speaks some French and whose strange beauty, reserved attitude, and passionate devotion intrigue us. After the prior has, I suppose, blessed the food, we sit down on the white wooden benches. The monks' hands are rough and calloused, swollen from working the fields, and their robustness is at one with the plates and enameled earthenware common to the country and implying the soil. Before each guest are three earthen bowls containing raw tomatoes, boiled beans, and fish, nothing else. And in front of him is a wine pitcher and a tin goblet, together with round, heavy black rye bread, the daily treasure, the meritorious symbol. In front of the apse, the superiors break the bread, eat their food and drink their wine from the earthen dishes and the green jugs on the unvarnished wood boards, and nothing more. A joyous atmosphere. Sun-burned faces smile in our direction, often with attempts at conversation but always without success! The frugal meal quickly dispatched, we rise and observe the brothers depart in procession, each of them saying some word to us, while many take our hands and kiss them.

This is the monastery of the working monks of Karakallou! Their frugal hospitality lingers on like a blessing. The good people of Karakallou! To this memory I add the one of my whitewashed room, where I slept on a wide bench rolled up on the most marvelous Bosnian or Walachian rug, blooming with colors. From the window lodged at the end of a deep splay, three times, I watch at dawn the light invade this endless space, while below, at the foot of the walls, the olive trees looked like tiny lichen.

How painful is this inability to record on paper the impression that the patches of earth, the perpendicularity of the red rocks, the expanse of the sea have stirred in the depths of my soul, without opening to them the light of day! Some crazy mules with rough and unexpected ways will sometimes send you tumbling sideways onto steep strands assaulted by the waves, simply by raising their backsides. The glaring presence of a white sun confuses one's sense of color. Hermits in their skete, one or two black, hairy, bearded monks, bow with kind or dumb smiles, their hands crossed on the chest, on the threshold of a hovel of dry stones. The monastery of Prodromos, the "Precursor,"[7] disappears, while, rocked about in the saddles of these savages, we continue on high up the hill amid the dried-up, contorted, bitter trees: in its fixed position this monastery looks like a mason's level, and it stretches out to follow horizons that aren't even there: today again the sea has neither substance nor boundaries.

Sturdy as a nutshell, a diminutive skiff bobs among the ephemeral space and streaks cheerfully on, not far from the shore and parallel to it; its ropes, a sail, and three fellows steer it to the right, to the pedestal of the land of Athos rising like an infinite pyramid capped with marble. The huge walls and battlements, a forbidding citadel, a monastery for servants of the Virgin! Go on, these people who jealously concealed their pious idleness, and these treasures were sent here as charitable offerings by workers from a diocese of orthodox and decadent Greece, or from wild Serbia, dedicated to the worship of the Greek cross. Pebbles, a cove, a mulberry tree with its trunk encircled by stones in the shape of a tiara piled high with soil that stains the sand around it with fruit so ripe that their juice trickles as they fall; a porch reached quite slowly once the ship's gear had been put away, beyond a court-yard around a church restored to its orthodoxy with a sheet metal roof, and icy corridors, huge bare guest rooms, the visit of the head priest, his table, the food—the illness, the gnawing stomach, the pain, the prostration, the inertia; the library seen between two intestinal attacks, and crazy mules overstuffed with oats, who prick up their curious ears and gallop off again.

"The fleet of Xerxes was annihilated at the foot of this immense rock," from whose top we examine with a shudder the frightening depths and the terrifying blackness of the bottomless sea.

Courage! you treasure seekers, go to it! The entire fleet of Xerxes, the conqueror, lies in frustrated wait under maybe two thousand meters of water. Upright red rocks.

The grass is cut clean by the crushing steps of our mules, and in its vertical and sharp fall it recalls the gigantic flute of a Delphic world. There is an implicit sense of catastrophe about it; even under such an extravagantly vivid sky as today's, I cannot imagine a rowboat venturing out on the smooth blue surface at the deep base of this spur: it would

*Courtyard of a monastery
on Athos (courtesy FLC)*

be struck with fear. God! Can you imagine the storm and its senseless onslaught, its wonderful spurting, titanic whoosh, whoosh! And there it is, the fleet of Xerxes, every anchor desperately plunging for a bottom that is nowhere to be found, blown sideways by that fury and striking the rock; the splintering of wood, the dry jetty, the crushed men, the oblique descent of the Persian warriors to the glaucous depths, eyes closed, mouths open—their landing on sands never stirred, unexpected visitors to regions supposedly calm. Up above, the effusive sky spouting water, the indescribable uproar of a sea in delirium, its inconceivable pounding against the enormous red buttress—on top of which our mules drag us, trotting along and plotting another sure trick. Salamanders await our arrival in the courtyard of a large skete; the monks come running:[8]

—Franzuski, we said.

—Ah, Franzuski!

Hands crossed on the chest, eagerness, joy in their faces. These folk are active hermits recently arrived from the Russian steppe, and France is a member of the Alliance.[9]

—Franzuski, ah Franzuski!

The table is set with red tomatoes and superabundant wine; we drank the customary resin wines; and here we go, on the back of Bacchus's donkey! Night falls, the sky full of stars, the smooth, tender sea filling the entire window frame. Another bottle of wine. As on so many evenings, as every evening on Athos, the warm and hospitable wine goes to our heads, and everything becomes pleasant; the illness subsides . . . for the night! We know it only too well, and also the anguishing mad rush along dark corridors until . . . Ah! Athos opens the doors of its monasteries; ah! Athos buzzes in its sketes with working monks and so joyful is their hospitality that it does the heart good! The wine of Athos excites my memory this evening!

The doleful evening of a day devoted to galling and unpardonably trivial discoveries, demonstrating the sad effects of living in a small town, brings to mind a vague but sweet memory, of melancholic uncertainty, of radiant unease. Here, at this hour, with a broad smile and a mouth filled with joy, I experienced again, like the distant cry of an unacknowledged loneliness, as when the two of us taking leave of one another feel a growing impulse—which, maybe, I alone felt—for a simple but ardent caress—a joy that my age and loneliness demand—at times—when a light, a smile or the sun, or some ineffable music, or the sweetness of the air and the season incite the body and its heart to a friendly testimonial of the most profound sympathy.

These memories of the East, appearing in their sunny splendor at four o'clock in the afternoon under the warm belly of the white sky, were exhausting my joys, drowning them in sorrow.

A call reverberates from the inner depths of my being and the disquieting images of that landscape, which I conjure up from memory this evening, pained my heart and shattered my mind. Luckily, the blinding light removed all the terror from the nightmare. At the sharply pointed peak of the pyramid of Athos, we experienced all around us a slight estrangement, and if, to get our bearings, we looked down into crevices cushioned with light and formed by the buttresses raised out of the sea, the utterly unknown image of a profile of land would appear detached, as if in ether. For the sea, sparkling with a white glitter, evades the searching eye and hollows out this strange void, which we perceive in a kind of waking nightmare, when fixing for ourselves a point of reference, we venture to imagine our world as it revolves in its atmosphere, tracing its path in infinite space. Thus, from the summit of the pyramid of Athos, a shadow was cast upon the sea all around us, except in the isthmus at the west, as if a body had fallen into this luminous immensity. In reality we are at the threshold of a small votive chapel, but I feel no emotion. Yet, located at the highest point on the land, the chapel of the Virgin must be like the unleavened bread of an ineffable communion for some of the pilgrims who have come this far. I assume that whoever has spent weeks at sea, and days going from monastery to skete and from skete to monastery to reach the one nearest the summit, that of St. George, and then having come with a guide, having ridden for hours over a savage and uninhabited terrain up to a refuge at the foot of the marble crest, having tied his mule next to a well and entrusted it to a discreet guide, having undertaken the final climb up the ultimate marble slope alone, and having with a final leap arrived upon the highest platform from which infinity seizes him—must break down in tears, must collapse into contemplation. Then I consider the significance of this unpretentious altar of white-washed earth with an icon on a simple cheap print and a tiny oil lamp that the pilgrim himself refills from a demijohn placed nearby, as if the chapel had been without worshippers for some time. So far out to sea, so high in the sky, and on the road to Jerusalem, we have really reached a sanctuary—as ultimate as the last notes of a modern symphony. The Orthodox faith, a greenhouse warm with mysticism, transports the faithful into beatitudes.

As for me, pushed to action by the demanding conviction of a builder who dreams of uniting steel with concrete in strong rhythms, I am happy to know that once upon a time a Zeus made of bronze stood upon this hill. The adventurous galleys skipped over the waves to the biting of the oars, and the captain, merchants, warriors, and conquerors, with a feeling of robust pride for the appearance of the huge pyramid of Athos with its virile seated god; meanwhile, as the slaves bent over their oars, a torrent of curses lent quite an impassive grandeur to these joyous seas where a mad race of shining dolphins seemed to weave a network that bound the ship's hull from the surface of the waves to the sea-green depths.

Between this powerful vision of epic times and the imperturbable secret of the Islamic peoples extending across all the brown surrounding lands, this orthodox presence of a monastic life, this Byzantinism emptied like an echoless chasm, moves me.

Returning down the two thousand meters of white marble and brown limestone brings us back again to the sea by way of the skete of Saint George and that of Saint Ann, as far as the icy monastery of Saint Paul, not far from that rocky cove where the mulberry tree let its overripe fruit drip. I would dearly like to leave this island! But we have to wait eight days before a ship will again drop anchor in these idle waters.

On a radiant morning, having crossed the entire ridge of the sphinxlike mountain, we descend into Rossikon, our mules guiding us down the steep paths of the vineyards.[10] To the left, a single plane tree rises up amid these vineyards as if in interpellation. It alone speaks of Persia. So much of its structure—its smooth trunk—is gray like black marble washed by rains. Its biggest branches spring forth like rays, and its smallest hang down like droplets from a fountain. Its leaves are not at all bushy but sparse, just as in the miniatures: one leaf after another, until the tree, like a big open hand, has all its fingers covered with a graceful jewelry of emeralds. Rising from its roots against the background of the sea, so much of this lone, elevated creature echoes like a distant sound, poetic, diffused, expressed with the graciousness of a tale from an Orient other than this one, in a golden aura like those ripples sparkling with lacquer over an earth pink as illuminated coral reefs, among blue vineyards and beneath a sky breaking through these slender leaves, a tale much sweeter and more tender, as in a dream.

---

From the outside only the parvis seems to be on a human scale. Blocking the sky, the scale of the detail at the front of the building, the added buttresses, the back view of the triumphal arches, and the dome, seen from close-up, formed a bewildering conglomeration. As soon as we had crossed over the threshold of the porch, the somber narthex revived our memories of the age of great builders, not so much by its marbles and the sparkle of its mosaics but through the bold and simple span of its vault, hollowed out like a sarcophagus. Within this penumbra the main door opened suddenly onto the luminous splendors of the immense nave. The span across formed an incredible void, a gigantic swell of interior space that pushed way up the transverse ribs, grafted with four bearing pendentives carrying to the beyond the horizontal crown of the infinite windows of the dome—its solemn bosom. Two things: the straightness of the nave, like an immense forum, and then the hollow onion bulb of the dome proclaim the miracle—the masterpiece—of man. Isidore of Miletus and Anthemius of Tralles, almost without precedent, invented this method of construction and these abutting members in the year 500 to achieve their dream.[11]

Following this imperial canticle, the eastern world remained silent for centuries, and the Byzantine soul, perpetuated to this day by the strange phenomenon of a madreporic vitality, has been crystallized in the sanctuarial forms of the "paraclete" and the "diocesan"—the miniscule churches—none other than those surrounded by their quadrilaterals of masonry within each monastery of Athos. The Hagia Sophia is to Constantinople, and the Seraglio on its promontory to the Marmara and the Golden Horn, what the pyramid of Athos is to Chalkidiki, a mountain.[12]

The monastic spirit of Athos, the hermits and the praying brothers, conceived the idea of a crypt, to enshrine in morbid gold their contemplations inside this severe and obscure vault darkened by the imagery of the sanctuary. But this architecture, however diminished in volume, commands my admiration, and I spend hours deciphering its firm and dogmatic language.

At one time the main route from Asia on the way to Syracuse, Perigord, and Spain, through Venice and Aix-la-Chapelle, passed through here, and revealed to the outside world its geometrical combinations, its interior pomp, and its sackcloth robes. I felt quite strongly that the singular and noble task of the architect is to open the soul to poetic realms, by using materials with integrity so as to make them useful. To provide the Mother of God with a house of stone sheltered from old misdeeds and to arrange the volumes of that sanctuary in such a way that a spirit emanates from it, inspiring through its mysterious relationships of form and color the respect of everyone, silence upon the lips, and fostering nothing but the rise of prayers and the singing of canticles in the rhythm of the controlled light—what a divine calling for the ancient builders! The purity of their purpose, of their efforts is lost. The discipline from now on is unknown to us, the bunglers of today. God! How painful was the ecstasy that seized us in

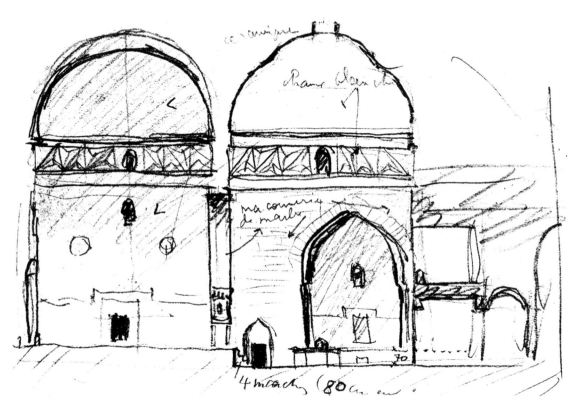

*Cross section of a small
Byzantine church (courtesy
FLC)*

those temples of the East! How withdrawn I felt, overcome by shame. Yet the hours spent in those silent sanctuaries inspired in me a youthful courage and the true desire to become an honorable builder. Unless you are a builder, you, the visitor who passes beneath the vaults of temples, cannot conceive the anguish of standing before these imperious verdicts in stone. We live in an age so lacking in scrupulous craftsmen, and heaven mercifully spares us from encounters with our predecessors: they would look upon us with dismayed astonishment; then they would hurl down their wrath upon us and put us to flight. The everpresent memory of their labor fills me with a gnawing anxiety and makes me dread each regulation according to which today, on our drawings, the works of architecture are built.

The Athos church is a concise model, comparable to a bud on a tree which, though very small before the warm spring rains, contains every treasure inside its firm and shining shield: for summer, the flower; for autumn, the fruit; and for winter, the slow and dark germination. There is a small dome—generally four meters—and placed in such a way that—from an open land that faces the sea, and perpetually swept by its breezes, and in the presence of the mountain—after crossing the narthex and a kind of pronaos, it appears big, self-sufficient, strong, and high; positioned like a hollow bulb seen through a telescopic tube, its drum seems surprisingly elevated; it is resting on four pendentives, themselves supported by four wide smooth arches that reach the ground through four simple, round, somewhat monolithic, gracefully curved shafts crowned by a trapezoidal capital. Leading the mind, the eye first observes the very dark pronaos where barrel vaults are suddenly pierced every now and then, to the left and the right, raising

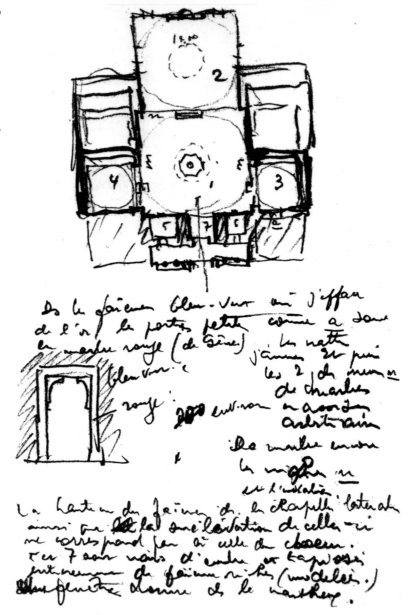

*Plan and detail of a small Byzantine church (courtesy FLC)*

dramatically the drum carrying the dome, then a taut surface luxuriously paved with a marble mosaic within the smooth walls of the enclosing quadrilateral and the four shafts supporting the vault, and in a dim, rich atmosphere darkened by the presence of innumerable frescoes, tarnished gold nimbuses interwoven with red ocher, ultramarine, green, and cobalt, recounting famous legends. The edifice is clearly articulated, in plan as well as in cross section, its mass both supporting and supported, its walls taut like muscles, and bulbs celebrating the curve. The powerful unity of its language is so sober that it confers to this impression the purity of a diamond. Hard and solid, it is the crystallization of a Hellenic clarity, mysteriously combined with undefinable Asiatic evocations.

Here are vestiges of paintings, deciphered in the darkness of the walls, which for the most part are cherished only later, after the deceptive signs of retouching and varnishing are washed away by time, and after the spirit of these things, relieved of its soiled envelope, has recovered the clarity of a majestic religiosity. Like a rosy apparition, in the corner of a pier stands, naive and youthful, the prince of some country—perhaps Serbia or Bulgaria. His posture is restrained, his toes joined together, seeming hesitant and anxious not to step forward. Against the darkened background of the fresco his two arms extend before him, presenting the model of a sanctuary—the very image of this church painted red with blue domes. His royal offering is made to a long-haired and bearded old man, the patriarch of this monastery, five times bigger than the prince, dressed in a rough black monk's robe and so faded that only the bowed and wrinkled head and the hands held out for the offering create a balanced contrast against the bright attire of the prince. Two tiny saints with gold and vermillion halos passing on a cloud barely touch them. Some Croatian prince who

A watercolor of a donor
prince presenting a patriarch with a model of a
church (courtesy FLC)

wished to ingratiate himself with God on the day of his ascension to the throne, must have built this sanctuary over there on Mount Athos, in which this dedicatory image was painted on the right side of its porch.[13]

I remember seeing a dreadful inferno in Lavras, its left wall covered by a raging fire. Emerging from an atrocious and terrifying mouth, gnashing its teeth, snorting its nostrils, tongues of flame rise upward like the red-ocher sea, tumbling and splashing, the infernal substance in a torrential vengeance, creating a nightmarish whirlpool in the tenebrous atmosphere. And many people like ourselves, naked and braying their laments, witness future calamities in that inferno where the "damned will be sent to burn."

But there is nothing as medieval in the vision of Filotheou: rather a Peri,[a] completely Hindu, Is seated on a creature of dreams, a dragon or a hippogriff. A lifted finger commands this ferocious rearing animal to silence.

Oh, no! right alongside it, I seem to recall some horrible disaster; an awful beast with several drooling heads, plunging into space, all its claws trying desperately to catch on to something, as the Peri falls with its arms outstretched. Could this possibly be some apocalyptic vision painted as a fresco by some man of Sassanian blood who has carried the painful nostalgia of Asiatic myth as far as this Christian sanctuary?[14]

Like a brocade, all the walls are covered from the peristyle to the pronaos, all the way up to the sanctuary. The imagery extends to the architraves and a decorative band of arcades, to the drums, as far as the domes. All the church dogmas are inscribed in them, as well as

a. This strange figure is a benevolent spirit in the East.

the legends and good deeds of men. There are ex-votos or acts of faith, all probably in an intentional and symbolic order, with each scene occupying its hierarchical place, and what's more, each subject and each figure painted to a predetermined size and scale in accordance with some strong, subtle meaning. Iconoclastic proscriptions have done away with all statuary forms. Sumptuous and garish paintings have invaded the walls to such an extent that only the authoritative language of major architectural forms and the absence of all mouldings enable the churches of Athos to remain strong and beautiful.

Add to this an iconostasis sparkling with its golds between the marble paving and the triumphal arch, hiding behind the wall all the legends of the Passion and isolating the secret of the apse. But being too tired, and not methodical enough (or not scientific enough), we visitors too hurried, and too distracted, did not examine these invaluable museums of Byzantine painting. Rather we often railed against the horrible restorations, turning our backs to the painted book open before our eyes, whose every page merited understanding and love.

So many things made us leave Athos in too much of a hurry: the libraries in total disorder, the librarians not even knowing what they had at their disposal (marvelous documents), the impossibility of making ourselves understood, the debilitating illness which sapped our energies. Yet I know I shall never return there. You have to be sitting alone in your room on a desperate, rainy Sunday in a sad provincial town to feel the anguish at having let so much happiness go by! The most vivid memory is clothed in purple, pink, and ultramarine and wears a radiant crown and a golden chasuble, and your spirit, a penitent pilgrim, crosses over lands and seas, returning to recover, almost intact, in some strangely exact sanctuary, emotions once lived.

But at his moment on my table I have a memento: a smeared drawing of a miniature, a few square centimeters in size, sketched in the library of the Rossikon monastery the morning of our departure from Athos. In the illumination, which was smaller than the palm of my hand, the most intensely green plain—I am reminded of the same malachite green that preceded the thunderstorm I saw one night in Ravenna on my way back from Saint Apollinare in Classe—was depicted under a golden sky as immense, smooth, and shimmering as that of icons.[15] A woman in a black robe, bowing in supplication, and represented in such archaic style, seems to emit a cry of abandon. There is a dark cloud in one corner, and some flowers, bent as the woman, under the intensity of a storm. What strange power for such an awkward little image, so small that there is room enough for the imagination, and we can't thank enough the naive illuminator, who, a thousand years ago, knew how to combine these three eloquent colors and how to create this willful unity of movement. A spiritual drama pervades this picture.

And since it speaks of power, an even more startling memory comes to my mind, of the great icon in the refectory of Iviron. It had an immense stone barrel vault, an entirely Roman structure with groined vaults that create a rhythmic pattern counteracting the thrust of the stonework. It was whitewashed, and the ground was partly paved. The tables consisted of enormous thick slabs of white marble. Every step echoed with solemnity in a hall so empty and white that the black monks moved about it not like volumes but more like spots or holes. High up on the wall terminating in an apse was a large icon framed in black. The gold background was tarnished, but a Virgin stood out more powerful than the one by Cimabue.

I think that a painting presented in this manner is very convincing, and not as monastic in spirit as those I saw in all the little churches plastered with frescoes, somewhat like cells enclosed in a monastery whose door hung with a portcullis opens onto a trench facing a drawbridge, a temple of men withdrawn into themselves and, having renounced all worldly contests, confined to their island which they dare not ever leave.

Oh, how closed in were those sanctuaries!

How much I like Hagia Sophia for belonging to innumerable Turks, conquered, it seems to me, in a bloody apotheosis on a golden evening by Mehmet the Conqueror who, there, in that immense and glorious nave of gold transparencies and enamels, left the breath of a great age, the great aura of subjugated nations and seas.

---

Morbid meditations.

During a festive night . . .

A fantastic vision of the sanctuary of the Virgin . . .

In a dark apse behind the iconostasis.

After a year of darkness the iconostasis is ablaze with brilliant golds rekindled by the fiery torch of offerings burning in the chancel.

The torch is in the shape of a conifer, with masses of superimposed flaming and dripping candles which the officiating priest impales every second at the demand of a pilgrim who came here through the night. Candles of pure golden wax. The moaning, the crying, the shouting, the gasping, the chanting, the dying melody of the liturgical phrase. The cadence, scherzo, and fugal march of the same phrase. The wavy and delicate intercessions subdued in the same phrase. The ceremonial music transcends the minds of those who are here; it rises above the burning tree and the heavy incense smoke, over the narrow and deep dome, across the frigid and pellucid starlit skies toward a remote abode.

Suddenly, I feel a contraction in my forehead, and my knees tremble to see, late in the night, the external forms of the sanctuary of the Virgin on Mount Athos and the monastery of Iberians at Iviron by the seashore.

The exterior is as red as iron reaching melting point. There it is, swollen, supple, and so close to the earth on the level shoreline, its pleasing oval forms radiant with clarity like an Egyptian alabaster urn carrying a burning lamp.

The urn is strangely protective this evening, as if in mystical abandon outright gifts are torn away from living flesh and offered in painful and bloody oblations to the Beyond, to the Other, to Whomever, to any Other than the self.

The overwhelming delirium of this moment and place. In the few moments of confusion in which you can no longer control yourself, the poignant sensation of feeling *absolutely* alone, in a crypt dedicated to the most passionate presence of worshipped divinity opens your chest, tortures your soul, tears open your heart, and hurls it, still beating, into the tree burning with the offerings of the pilgrims and embellished by their prayers.

It seemed to me that the complete atmosphere, the clouds as well as the incommensurate space beyond, were black and bereft of light. And having partaken of the spiritual mood, having come from so far and arrived at last at this place, I felt in my limbs the awe of the sacred ritual!

At the edge of the dark sea the sand and the waves meet glittering alabaster shells—five little shells, five little domes, and then small apses, the joining of the transverse arches to the vaulted porch offset by the cylindrical interpenetration, all animated by a crowd of people going in and out, a crowd gathered in the courtyard, a crowd seated in the refectories, and the four penumbral wings of the Monastery of Iviron, enclosed around the sanctuary with their outside façades turned toward the night, three toward the sea, one toward the mountain.

For hours we endured the continuous and monotonous unfolding of the ceremony, standing in the pew to which Brother Chrysanthos had taken us. Chrysanthos took his place at our left and began to chant.

An extreme fatigue makes me hallucinate. Just think: after climbing down a mountain all afternoon in the painful heat, and starving, we had to provide an explanation for our return to this monastery which we had left six days before:

—We have come for the festival of the Virgin, we have come for the music, for the rituals, to exalt with you, with all the goodwill we can pledge to you.

We were dying of hunger, but Chrysanthos, not even giving it a thought, quite simply and in a friendly way pushed us into the church, opening for us a passage in the darkness, dense and packed with a crowd of pilgrims, and gave us the place of honor in the transept within the furnace of incense opposite the bishop and immediately beside the large empty space dominated by the iconostasis where the tree of candles was burning—since we had returned for the music, the rituals.

Midnight passed, raising our spirits. Standing in the pews, we became consumed by exhaustion. Two o'clock came. Pushed to the limits, poor old men slumped on their knees, drowsy and shrunken. We were dying of hunger, right alongside the altar, waiting for all this to end. Then, the music intensified its raking of our senses; wandered, my mind wandered, reliving in flashes forgotten moments of my pathetic existence, and I counted all the countries covered in darkness that separated me from the roofs under which my friends and family lay sleeping! And whereas all sleep like the dead, what is it, this diabolical mystical frenzy panting under these vaults, which a little while ago I dreamed to be a view of heaven, where prayers ought to end in the form of a warm tabernacle, as delicate as the alabaster urn animated by the flame of an oil lamp?[16]

The bishop of Salonika, who came especially for this occasion, dressed in purple, presides over this service in the crypt—like a Hindu vision of a bygone age, of extinct races, and of terrifying cults. The bishop will stand in attendance without speaking or moving until morning, apparently with a mission to remain here as an emissary from heaven. The silence brought on by the somnolence of the majority—some dozing off in their places, others in the corners of the courtyard or crowded on benches in the hallways—gives the remaining participants the feeling of an important function to perform: dawn must find the church ablaze with prayers! *Muezzins* crying out high up in their towers in the afternoon light are nothing like this; nor did the dervishes in Scutari have such a sweet and piercing frenzy: these are cries of the heart, cries of wild beasts, and howls. Swollen temples appear about to burst; the veins of crimson foreheads bulge out like ropes and gnarled cables. Those four or five who obstinately continue the chanting, with stubborn, uniform, passionate cries, raise their convulsed faces to the darkness of the dome, leaning against the railings of the pews. A great peace surrounds us, we who are immeasurably distressed; the night, the sea, the mountain—and we with the loud clamor of cries calling in anguish from beneath the domes permeated by the smoke of the wax and the incense. Finally, closing my eyes, I have a vision of a black shroud covered with golden stars. In fact I am in the shroud, but a stranger to the stars!

Like a mannequin I am dragged toward the refectory.

---

Irritation, long repressed, strains and builds up, until at last it will explode. Petty monks, crenellated walls, anachronistic fortresses, menials—also the rifraff—or angelic beauty, and the confinement and the sugary pilgrims, enraptured sugar plums, banqueters, and those two indescribably kind monks at Karakallou; Brother "Gold Flower," so reserved and so secretly coquettish so as to reveal the true measure of his genuine and beautiful superiority—ah, I've had enough of all the sweetness of that nature, swollen with sap, damp with joy, quivering with abundant vines, all of it eternally, daily, parading before an immutable sea, bringing and carrying away the ecstatic and venal pilgrims! Not a single woman is to be seen; thus everything is missing here in the East where, if only for the sight of her, woman is the primordial ingredient. Nor does one see battles, skirmishes, or wars erupting but only attacks of cunning language, over in the dreary hall of the *protos,* or among the nine *epistates,* with the faces of hyenas or of incurable Amfortas.[17]

One sees no children! Never would I have thought myself capable of this remark! And what is more, to be affected by it! Nor baby chickens, nor baby donkeys, nor doves.[18]

All are lonely males, and if not consumed by anguish, then devoid of any noble martial feeling. What are they then? Within the growing malaise of the body, the brain, while cogitating, compiles and aggravates the malaise. Then, should I remain? No! I must flee the sacred mountain and its disquieting sweetness, or else, like those holy brothers of Karakallou, I shall slave in the wheat fields, the hazelnut groves, the olive orchards, or I shall whitewash the walls or the hallways. Not quite, because in the evening, hands dangling between the thighs, eyes, guided by thoughts, would be cast . . . on the brothers, ah torment, sad sojourn in Athos. Yet there rebels in me a feeling of gratitude, affection, and so on.

Inexorable sun, overwhelming immutable sea, so much, much too much. Oh, to struggle, to move, to cry, to create!

---

In the drowsiness of everything, in the vague intoxication of feeling space collapse and expand; in the turmoil of unconscious projects, of wonderful hopes, the ship casts off, glides, whips the water, faces the open sea, plunges into it, resolutely heading south. And we, sleeping on our backs among so many different kinds of people, we see, entirely blue under the full moon still hidden behind an immense marble trihedral, the Holy Pyramid, dominating us and offering to our scrutinizing view its sides clustered with fortresses, of black monks, walls, and battlements.

And then, the incomparable calm and the tragic latency of the eastern soul rises up from throats and nostrils, in sad songs, chants, recitatives, litanies, and cries. All this accompanied by a very strange big and beautiful guitar, and amid all those song lovers who listen respectfully and who are our very numerous and unknown traveling companions. On this freighter, which belongs to a company that makes no distinction of class, the crew, reduced to a minimum, mingles with us and listens. Some of them are going to Jerusalem; some are fleeing Lódz and Kiev. There are Persians and Caucasians going to Mecca. Others toward America, escaping Turkish conscription—a crowd of nineteen-year-olds. All of us on this strange boat, including those of us who are going to see the Acropolis, all of us haunted by a dream, a yearning, a madness.

Night falls, black and gentle over our field of vision. Mount Athos has disappeared. But how many stars there are!

# THE PARTHENON

I shall give this entire account an ocher cast, for the earth is free of greenery and appears to be of baked clay. Black and gray stones will teeter-totter terrifyingly on immense reaches confined only by craggy rocks or restrained by the rugged mountain slopes. Their harsh forms, softened by neither sea nor time, will penetrate numerous inlets and erode their edges at the outermost bounds of vast red expanses, harsh and barren. Such is the spectacle at each step along the way from Eleusis to Athens.

The everpresent sea, pale at noon, blazing at twilight, serves as a measure for the height of the mountains that obstructs the horizon. The compressed landscape thus no longer benefits from the infinite space that softened the imagery of Athos. The Acropolis—this rock—rises alone in the heart of an enclosed frame. Slightly to the left beyond Piraeus, where vapors rise from the sea, one senses that the open sea is just beyond and that flotillas enter there. Hymettus and Pentelicus, two very high mountain ranges, like two wide adjoining screens, are located behind us, orienting our sight in the opposite direction, toward the estuary of stone and sand, the Piraeus. The Acropolis, whose flat summit bears the temples, captivates our attention, like a pearl in its shell. One collects the shell only for its pearl. The temples are the cause of this landscape.

What light!

At noon I saw the mountains shimmering just like hot air over a basin of molten lead.

A shady spot stands out like a hole. Here one sees no half-shadows at all. The uniformly red landscape is reflected by the temples. Their marbles have the luster of new bronze against the azure sky. Close-up, they really seem as reddish brown as terra-cotta. Never in my life

*Temples on the Acropolis*
*(courtesy Jean Petit)*

*The Parthenon, "a sovereign cube facing the sea" (courtesy FLC)*

have I experienced the subtleties of such monochromy. The body, the mind, the heart gasp, suddenly overpowered.

Here, the rectitude of the temples, their impeccable structure and the brutality of the site were confirmed. The strong spirit triumphs. Too lucidly the herald blows a brazen trumpet and proffers a jarring blast. The entablature of a cruel rigidity crushes and terrorizes. The feeling of a superhuman fatality seizes you. The Parthenon, a terrible machine, grinds and dominates; seen from as far as a four-hour walk and one hour by boat, alone it is a sovereign cube facing the sea.

After weeks of being crushed by this brutal site, I wished for a storm to come and drown in its floods and swirls the biting bronze of the temple.

When the storm did come, I saw through the large drops of rain the hill becoming suddenly white and the temple sparkling like a diadem against the ink-black Hymettus and the Pentilicus ravaged by downpours!

---

It has been a hot day. The awning, which is stretched out over the ship's prow where we were sitting, imprisoned the air. We struck up an acquaintance with two Russian mathematicians, women with mannish figures, strong features, and big eyes. They like to talk. Hours pass without reading or scribbling. Evening must be approaching because the chef can be seen bringing in dishes of dainty fried octopus—the octopus from Mycenae. We get up and sit on the ropes. We slip down a steel ladder into the kitchen to get some water, which we have to pump by hand, and also to draw an excellent Sicilian wine from a cask. Our gallant cook is from Syracuse; we declare to him:

—*Diavolo, il vino e buono!*

That's about all we know in Italian, but the man is pleased. On the way up, we brush past bulls tied between decks.

In Salonika the day before yesterday, at midnight, by a beautiful moonlight, eight hundred of them were loaded on board. Eight hundred bulls from Thessaly. As they arrived, they were shoved in between the stockades. The joints of the crane grated; the powerful hook dropped rapidly down to their heads. Quick, a running noose around the horns, brief command, the hook is taken up again carrying away that enormous mass of meat hung by its horns. A large arc was inscribed; the mechanism released the chain; like a pot, the bull arrived at the end of the hold and fell on its back, rolling its bewildered eyes. It hardly had time to recover when, seized by the ring in its muzzle, it was firmly fastened. In the lair of the hold a hanging lantern barely illuminated the sharp silhouettes of the two bold cowherds.

Once the sky completed its metamorphosis, the last burst of green died away on the water. A star finds some receptive facet of a wave to reflect. The deck has emptied, and there are only three or four of us remaining. With Auguste regularly tamping his pipe, it's a moment of pleasure. A tenderness prevails; the memory of the East that I love so revolves in my mind, intermingled with those golden skies seen in the icons. My eyes are riveted on the same horizon, always similar. All is at rest. There is still a last brief meeting of the ship's officers, followed by the monotonous pace of the lookout high up on the bridge. Through the windows of the bridge, we can glimpse the rudder turned by the effort of two men: the only throbbing heart at this hour when everything else is asleep.

All my nights at sea I spent under the stars, wrapped in a multicolored rug from Rumania purchased at the monastery of Prodromos on Mount Athos. What sweeter litany can there be than that of the bow waves slapping against a hull vibrating with the ship's engines. Noises of movements to and fro disturb the silence of this night. Before daybreak we shall enter between the shores. With a silent patience, the big boat has steamed without respite for the last two days. The land of Euboea is on the starboard side, a long dark ridge. We converse, Auguste and I, in low voices, and we feel a true excitement to think that by this evening we shall have seen the immortal marbles.

For a long time the prow has pivoted on the hinge of the rudder; land surrounds us everywhere except behind us, where the sea threads its way into it. Here is Attica, and there is the Peloponnesus. Here is a white lighthouse and, very near, a harbor; here are unusually jagged hills, little resembling those of Broussa or the ones behind Scutari. The sea is deserted; at this moment of dawn there are none of the countless longboats laden with carpous, tomatoes, and vegetables, which, as in Constantinople, are heading toward the city with the clumsy haste of big beetles. This brown land seems a desert. Very far away in the center of the harbor, at the bosom of some hills forming an arch, a strange rock stands out, flat at the top and secured on its right by a yellow cube. The Parthenon and the Acropolis! But we cannot believe it; we don't give it a thought. We are bewildered; the ship does not enter the harbor but continues on its course.

The symbolic rock disappears, hidden by a promontory. The sea is extremely narrow; we pass around an island. Oh, damn! Ten, twenty ships are anchored there, each flying a yellow flag! The flag of cholera, that of the Kavas; from the Black Sea to Tuzla on the Marmara. That flag we know indeed! The propeller suddenly becomes silent. The anchors drop. We stop. The yellow flag is hoisted. Stupefaction! A great stir, general restlessness. The captain is nervous, becomes violent, shouts, insults:

—The longboats are in the water. Passengers for Athens, come on, get moving!

Chaos. Bundles and boxes, men and women, come clattering down the ladder. Such cries, such insults, such shouting, and in every language. On a small pier toward which the oarsmen steer us is a gentleman with a white cap, servile with the rich, brutal and rude with the poor: a functionary, a penpusher! Wire fences separate the barracks. The quarantine!

A stinking quarantine on a desolate island about the size of a public square. A stupid quarantine, administrated against all the laws of common sense; a hotbed for cholera, this quarantine. Here, the functionaries, over there, the thieves, the dishonest; a disgrace to the Greek government that established it. For four days they held us there, to sleep with strangers, vermin, and earwigs under a burning sky without a single tree to lessen the hardship upon this devil's island. A restaurant—what a pompous title—a swindling place, where those who run it, a deputy, so they say, allow a liter of water to be sold for forty centimes and force you to eat garbage at scandalous prices. Ah, how do the poor manage—those for whom a drachma is a fortune?[a]

That was on the Island of St. George, in the Bay of Salamis, facing Eleusis. O time, annihilate this vile epoch! This was our first acquaintance with you, epic places, degraded by so-called descendants. Our complaints recorded in the travelers' log book of the island were unanimous. But no, a blind and narrow patriotism scribbled alongside childish and dithyrambic praises signed Papapoulos, Danapoulos, Ni-

a. The drachma was worth one franc. As reference: at the time (in 1911) after five months of travel from Prague to Athens, I spent 800 francs which included my camera supplies.

kolesteos, Phytanopoulos, among others. This was enough to ensure immunity to the administrators of this infamy and, who knows, maybe an honorary recompense.

———————

Fever shook my heart. We had arrived at Athens at eleven in the morning, but I made up a thousand excuses not to climb "up there" right away. Finally, I explained to my good friend Auguste that I would not go up with him. That anxiety gripped me, that I was in a state of extreme excitement, and would he "please" leave me alone. I drank coffee all afternoon absorbed in reading the voluminous five-week-old mail picked up at the post office. Then I walked the streets waiting for the sun to go down, wishing to finish the day "up there" so that, once I came down again, I could only go to bed.

To see the Acropolis is a dream one treasures[b] without even dreaming to realize it. I don't really know why this hill harbors the essence of artistic thought. I can appreciate the perfection of these temples and realize that nowhere else are they so extraordinary; and a long time ago I accepted the fact that this place should be like a repository of a sacred standard, the basis for all measurement in art. Why this architecture and no other? I can well accept that according to logic, everything here is resolved in accordance with an unsurpassable formula, but why is it that the taste—or rather the heart that guides people and dictates their beliefs despite their tendency to ignore it at times—why is it still drawn to the Acropolis, to the foot of the temples? This is in my case an inexplicable problem.[1] For how much have I been

b. We are in 1911.

already led by an absolute enthusiasm for the works of other peoples, other times, other places! Yet why must I, like so many others, name the Parthenon the undeniable Master,[2] as it looms up from its stone base, and yield, even with anger, to its supremacy?

And this certainty, already foreseen even as I was bestowing all my unreserved admiration on Islam, was to be expressed this evening with the formidable strength of trumpets blasting from a hundred mouths like the noise of a waterfall. Yet recalling that Stamboul, from which I had expected so much, had not yielded up its secret until after twenty days of longing and working at it, I had within me, as I passed through the Propylaea, the deliberate skepticism of someone who inevitably expects the most bitter disillusion.

As by the violence of a combat, I was stupefied by this gigantic apparition. Beyond the peristyle of the sacred hill, the Parthenon appeared alone and square holding high up above the thrust of its bronze-colored shafts its entablature, its stone brow. The steps below served as its support and increased its height by their twenty risers. Nothing existed but the temple, the sky, and the surface of paving stones damaged by centuries of plundering. And no other external sign of life was evident here, except, far off in the distance, Pentelicus, creditor of these stones, bearing in its side a marble wound, and Hymettus, colored the most opulent purple.

Having climbed steps that were too high, not cut to human scale, I entered the temple on the axis, between the fourth and the fifth fluted shafts. And turning back all at once from this spot once reserved for the gods and the priest, I took in at a glance the entire blazing sea and the already obscure mountains of the Peloponnesus, soon to be bitten

*The Parthenon seen from
the Propylaea (courtesy
FLC)*

*The stylobate of the Parthenon (courtesy FLC). One of thirteen watercolors exhibited under the title "Langage de Pierre" in Munich, (1911), Neuchâtel (1912), Zurich (1913), and Paris (at the Salon d' Autômne, 1913)*

by the disc of the sun. The steep slope of the hill and the higher elevation of the temple above the stone slabs of the Propylaea conceal from view all traces of modern life, and all of a sudden, two thousand years are obliterated, a harsh poetry seizes you. Dropping down onto one of those steps of time, head sunk in the hollow of your hand, you are stunned and shaken.

With its last rays the setting sun will strike this front of metopes and smooth architrave, and passing between the columns, crossing the open door at the back part of the portico, it would have awakened the shadow, hiding deep within the roofless cella, had it not long since been dispersed.

Standing on the highest step of the north side of the temple, right where the columns end, I observe that the horizontal is in line with the bay of the Aegina. Above my left shoulder the illusory wall composed of the repeated sharp fluting of the shafts soars to a tremendous height, assuming the appearance of a gigantic armor plate with the guttae of the mutules looking like its rivets.

At the very moment the sun touches the earth, a shrill whistle drives the visitor away, and the four or five[c] people who have made the pilgrimage to Athens cross again over the white threshold of the Propylaea and pass through the three portals. Pausing before the stairwell and impressed by this abyss of darkness, they hunch their shoulders as they sense, sparkling and elusive above the sea, a spectral past, an ineluctable presence.

c. It was the year of the great cholera epidemic in the East, and no foreigner dared to go there.

*The outer side of the Pro-*
*pylaea, the monumental*
*entrance of the Acropolis*
*(courtesy FLC)*

*The Temple of Athena
Nike (Wingless Victory)
"keeping watch at the
top of an ashlar stone
pedestal twenty meters
high" (courtesy FLC)*

The Temple of Wingless Victory, keeping watch at the top of an ashlar stone pedestal twenty meters high, lords over the orange surface of the sea on its left and silhouettes against the blazing sky the ionic shaft at the corner of its pronaos. The gracefully cut stones are dedicated to Victory. To calm my excitement, there remains a delightful twilight and the long stroll along the avenues of the clear and gay city, at the side of a good friend who on this first evening will respect willingly the tacit agreement of silence and encroaching peace.

---

The enclosing slopes at the top of the hill bind, by their steps, the temples and thrust their diversely spaced columns to the sky. Down the slope of the hill, steps leading to the Parthenon are cut out of the rock itself, presenting a first barrier. But huge marble steps hang above them, a certain obstacle to the approach of man. Priests came out of the cella, sensing the bosom of mountains behind them and sideways, and under the portico, they would cast a horizontal glance above the Propylaea at the sea and at the distant mountains it washes.

In the middle of the estuary at the bottom of which stands a temple, the sun charts its course until dusk, and in the sultry heat of the evening its disc touches the ground on the very axis of the temple. The crown of stone that marks the bounds of the plateau has that ability to dispel any inkling of life. Bewildered, the active mind grasps and plunges into a past that should not be reconstructed. But it would also be beautiful if, outside reality—these temples, this sea, these mountains, all this stone and water—could become for one hour only the heroic vision of a creative mind. What a thing!

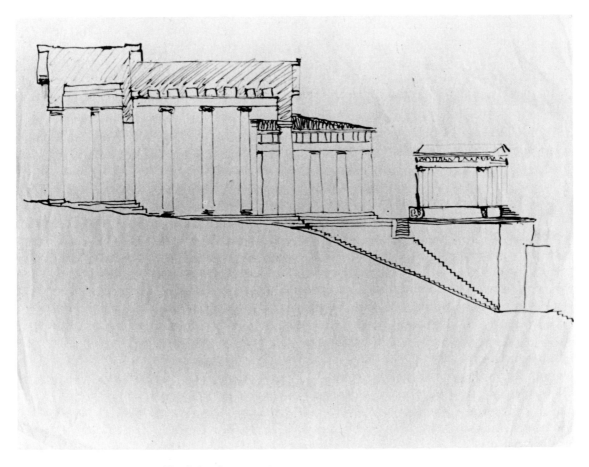

*The flight of stairs cut into
the slope of the hill leading
to the Propylaea and Par-
thenon (courtesy FLC)*

*The inner side of the*
*Propylaea seen from the*
*Parthenon (courtesy FLC)*

Physically, the impression is that of a most profound inspiration that expands your chest. It is like an ecstasy that pushes you onto the bare rock devoid of its old slab paving and, out of joy and admiration, throws you from the Temple of Minerva to the Temple of Erechtheum, and from there to the Propylaea. From beneath this portico, the Parthenon can be seen on its domineering block, casting in the distance its horizontal architrave and facing this concerted landscape with its front like a shield. The friezes still remaining above the cella show agile horsemen racing. I see them with my myopic eyes, way up there, as clearly as if I were touching them, because the depth of their reliefs is so well proportioned to the wall that supports them.

The eight columns obey a unanimous law, soaring from the ground, not at all appearing to have been placed section by section by man, but instead giving the impression that they rise from the innermost depths of the earth; and the violent upsurge of their fluted surface brings to a height which the eye cannot estimate the smooth band of the architrave that rests on its abacus. The austere aggregate of metopes and triglyphs under the riveting of guttae carries the eye to the left corner of the temple, up to the farthest column of the opposite side, enabling the beholder to seize at a glance a single block, a gigantic prism of marble cut from bottom to top with the rectitude of clear mathematics and the precision that a machinist brings to his labor. Yet the western pediment with its peak projecting in the middle of the space—in harmony with the mountains, the sea, and the sky—strengthens the facade and its unmovable orientation.

I had thought it possible to compare this marble to new bronze, hoping that, in addition to the color so described, this word would suggest the pronounced luster of this substantial mass fixed in place with the

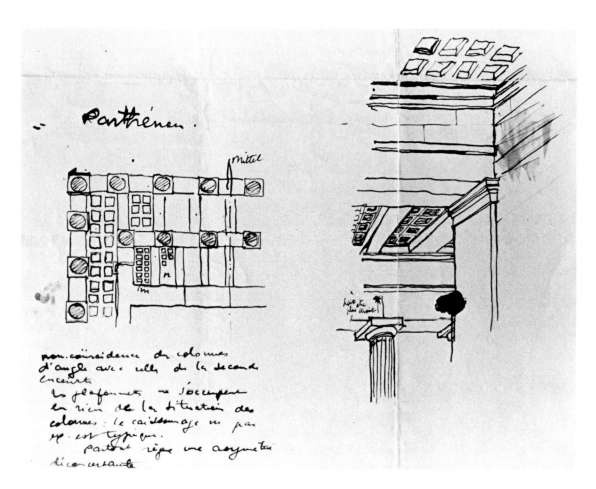

*Details of the Parthenon's ceiling and columns (courtesy FLC)*

inexorability of an oracle. In the face of the unexplainable intensity of this ruin, increasingly an abyss separates the soul which feels from the mind which measures.

A hundred paces away, welcomed by this inconquerable titan, smiles the lively temple with four faces—the Temple of the Erechtheum—atop a base of smooth walls with animated, fleshy marble blossoms. Ionic is its order—Persepolitan, its architraves. They say it was once inlaid with gold, precious stones, ivory, and ebony; the Asia of sanctuaries by some bewitching spell had cast these steely glances into confusion, taking advantage of the fact that the temple had once dared to smile. But thank God, time got the better of it, and from the hill I salute the reconquered monochrome. Facing the Parthenon which has already been described, one must point out the posture of six draped women who support the stone entablature where, for the first time, dentils appeared in Attica. Strangely stern and thoughtful women who smile and appear stiff, and yet seem to quiver—they stand here as perhaps the most concrete sign of opulence and prominence. Thus this cheerful temple with four faces presents a different portion to each patch of sky. Friezes with water lilies and acanthus leaves, combined with a palm leaf, a supernatural element, decorate it. Plug holes, still clearly visible upon the band of the architrave, indicate where a famous sequence of victories in the postures of dancers once adorned it. These marbles chiseled with high reliefs lie in some museum, but I don't remember which one. As for the north facade, which overhangs the enormous cliff of the hill bound off here by vertical walls of Piraeus stone interspersed with the drums of ancient columns, I don't know of a term that could express the ingenuous elegy of this tetrastyle

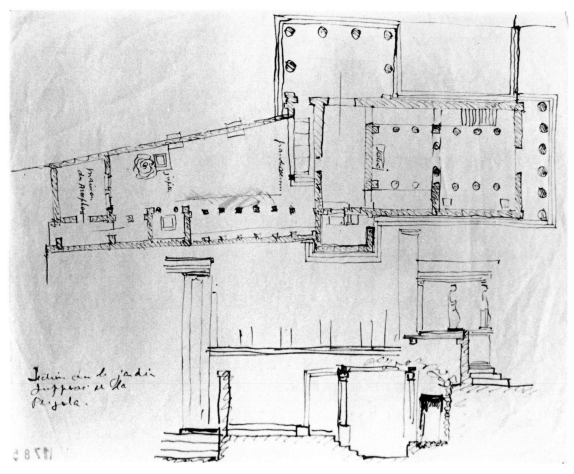

*Plan and section of the Er-
echtheum showing the cary-
atid porch (courtesy FLC)*

portico.[3] But having rested, I still prefer to go back to the Propylaea, amid the debris strewn on the ground, and, under that aegis of stones recently reassembled, to scrutinize the Parthenon.

Days and weeks passed in this dream and nightmare, from a bright morning, through intoxicating noon, until evening, when the sudden whistle of the guards would tear us away from all this, and cast us out beyond the wall pierced by three huge portals which, as I have said, overlook a growing darkness.

---

It's good that we other builders know and meditate on this place. Today, the temples of the Acropolis are twenty-five hundred years old. They have not been maintained for the last fifteen centuries. Not only have storms loosed their usual downpours, but, more harmful than earthquakes, men, troglodytes, have inhabited the hill certainly amazed by their good luck. And they have torn away whatever they needed, the marble slabs and the huge blocks, and have built any old way with mud and rubble shanties for swarms of children. The Turks used it as a fortress. What a target for an assault! One fine day in 1687 the Parthenon was used as a depository for explosives. During an attack an artillery shell hit the roof and ignited the gunpowder. Everything blew up.

The Parthenon has remained, torn apart but not jostled, and here it is: if you look for the joints between the twenty sections of drums comprising the fluted columns, you won't find them, even by running a fingernail over these areas, which can only be differentiated by the slight irregularities in the patina that each marble has collected over time;[4] your nail feels nothing. Properly speaking, the joint doesn't exist, and the sinewy rib of the fluting continues as though cut from a single stone!

Get down flat on your stomach in front of a shaft of the Propylaea and examine its foundation. First of all, you are upon paved ground whose horizontality is as absolute as a hypothesis. Made of huge slabs, the alabaster mass is set also upon an artificial ground, a deep foundation, or, better, a daring hoist. The base of the shaft, carved with twenty-four flutes, is as untarnished as the admiration you derive from it. The slab, chiseled all around like a bowl, reveals a difference in level of two or maybe three millimeters. This subtle detail executed two thousand years ago—a halo marking the base—is still perceptible, and as fresh and flawless as if the sculptor had only yesterday carried away the hammer and chisel that shaped this marble.

The wall with three portals, the center one opening widest so that the chariots could pass through during the Panathenaic festivals, has a marble surface of thousands of quarried stones fitted together so exactly that it induces a caress, and the hand, spread wide, wants to penetrate the mirage of its thousand-year-old layers. The surface as polished as a mirror plays with the contrasting veins that each quarrystone presents. Oh, but let us not examine these fragments hurled from the explosion! Like me, you will be defeated by this incomparable art and overwhelmed by shame. . . thinking about what we do, we others in the twentieth century.

To the left of the Parthenon entire columns are lying thrown down to the ground, like a man who receives gunpowder right in the face. Their drums are spread out like the links of a broken chain. If one has not seen them, one cannot imagine what these columns are like, and one does not grant them the grandeur that Ictinos vested in them.

Their diameter exceeds the heights of a man, the colossal scale used for an acropolis in a deserted landscape beyond any scale common to man. Incidentally, it is inconceivable that this scale would be also the one used by certain runts in our central Europe, the bastards of Vignola! Under the uniform architrave, an eloquently plastic mass that transfers the entire load of the entablature to the shaft, the barely curved echinus of the capitals is connected by three annulets whose total dimension is reduced to the size of a thumb. Each of these annulets (you see on the ground that overthrown capital) has dimensions measured in millimeters in relation to the fillets and flutings, which the slightest alteration would utterly destroy. Thus, having perceived these unprecedented truths among the ruins (useful evidence), it is a beautiful thing to examine them under the shadow of the cornices[d] and to verify their indispensable function.

Painstaking hours spent in the revealing light of the Acropolis. Perilous hours, provoking heartrending doubt in the strength of our strength, in the art of our art. It is obvious that an overwhelming Hellenism is precisely what is being described here, and the names of Ictinos, Callicrates, and Phidias are associated with the annulets of the echinus as they are with the supreme mathematics of the temple.[5]

Those who, while practicing the art of architecture, find themselves at a moment in their career somewhat empty-headed, their confidence

d. More then twenty meters high. (At the beginning of the first journey to the East, I wasn't yet accustomed to taking exact measurement of objects that attracted my attention. In any case an awareness of dimensions struck me soon after. From that time came what I called "the man with upraised arms," the key to all architecture.)

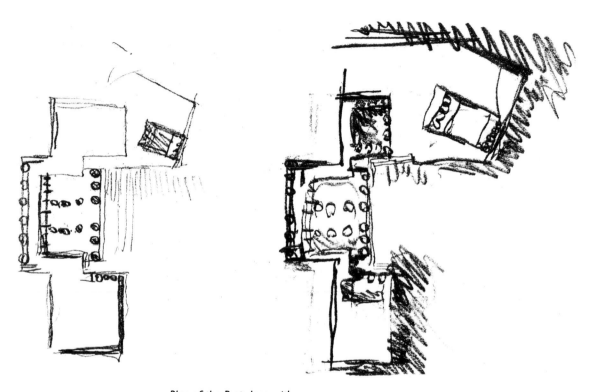

*Plan of the Propylaea with
Temple of Athena Nike
(Wingless Victory) in the
upper right (courtesy FLC)*

depleted by doubt before that task of giving a living form to inert matter, will understand the melancholy of my soliloquies amid ruins— and my chilling dialogues with silent stones. Very often, I left the Acropolis burdened by a heavy premonition, not daring to imagine that one day I would have to create.

———————

Many an evening from a side of Lycabettus that overlooks the Acro- polis, I could see beyond the modern city lighting up, the disabled hull[6] and its marble vigil—the Parthenon—dominating it, as if it were taking it toward the Piraeus, to the sea that had been the sacred route by which so many conquered treasures came to be laid out beneath the porticoes of the temples. Like a rocky hull, a giant tragic carcass in the dying light above all this red earth. A fading light upon the aridity of the red earth coagulates black blood about the Acropolis and its temple—the impassive pilot that maintains the course with all the movement of its outstretched sides. A serpentine light ignites an open boulevard winding around the giant tragic carcass and runs on the right toward public squares animated by modern life.

Here is truly a most infernal sight: a faltering sky extinguishing itself in the sea. The Peloponnesian mountains await the shadow to disappear, and as the night is clinging to all that is steadfast, the entire landscape suspends itself to the horizontal line of the sea. The dark knot that binds the sky to the darkened earth is that black pilot of marble. Its columns, springing out of the shadow, carry the obscure front, but flashes of light spurt out between them like the flames that would leap out of the portholes of a blazing ship.

———————

Today, I crossed again an immense landscape covered with rubble. I must have drunk much too much resin wine[e] to hold at bay the cholera of 1911 that was sweeping all the East. In the torpor of the land, a bay came into view, formerly dedicated to the mysteries: Eleusis! My imagination recreates to these ancient relics the eternal dialogue between architraved marbles and the horizons of the sea. Outsider, the visitor looks on. The sky is black. As if from the hollow of a huge overturned crucible, floods of bronze pour into the gulfs and the bays, and a few islands float on the sea like slag. A small train took me across some cultivated land. Soon we were at the top of a hill. Flocks of clouds weigh down like heavy balloons over the semicircular bay; three pine trees twisted in a desert of sand. The far-off mountains, with jagged edges tearing the pink fan of the last rays, were helping the green of the night to penetrate with its bitter vapors the quivering mass of the sky.

I caught a chill that completely sobered me up. I had been alone for many days now, and for seven months I have been traveling across Europe, from Berlin to here. My illness made me weak. I would spend every evening in a noisy café where the shrill sounds of violins would tear at my heart. Here it comes again, this music of stylish cafés and houses of ill-repute, the ineluctable signs of European progress.[7]

Again today I imbibed too much resin wine. In the streets I saw dead bodies being carried away, faces exposed, green and covered with flies; and black robed Orthodox priests.[8]

e. Resin wine in the East is an ancestor of absinthe, a drink prohibited in France since the day the First World War was declared.

Every hour it grows more deadly up there. The first shock was the strongest. Admiration, adoration, and then annihilation. But it disappears and escapes me; I slip in front of the columns and the cruel entablature; I don't like going there any more. When I see it from afar it is like a corpse. The feeling of compassion is over. It is a prophetic art from which one cannot escape. As insentient as an immense and unalterable truth.

But when I come upon a drawing of Stamboul in my sketch book, it warms my heart!

---

Today, my message is more dignified. Flipping through thousands of photographs arranged in folders at the Archeological Institute, I saw a picture of the three pyramids. The magnitude of the wind that shapes dunes has swept from my mind the anguish of the Oedipus. The extreme commotion of these many weeks is dissipating: I have easy things, known architectures, and I dream of a spot in Italy, of a Carthusian monastery.[9]

My mind is made up; I shall not tackle a new culture. The gesture of the pyramids is too large, and I'm too weary. The next stop will be the Cape of Calabria, and not Cyprus. I shall see neither the Mosque of Omar nor the pyramids.

And yet I write with eyes that have seen the Acropolis, and I will leave with joy.

Oh!

Light!

Marbles!

Monochromy!

*Cleobis and Biton, early sixth century B.C., sketched at the Museum of Delphi in 1911 (courtesy FLC)*

Pediments all abolished but not the one on the Parthenon, the contemplator of the sea, a block from another world. It takes a man and places him above the world. Acropolis that fulfills, that exalts![10]
The joy of remembering seizes me, and it is uplifting to carry away the sight of such things as a new part of my being, hereafter inseparable.

*Views of the landscape between Patras and Missolonghi, Greece (courtesy FLC)*

à l'opposé

# IN THE WEST[1]

I am greatly moved by everything in Italy. I had lived four months in great simplicity: the sea, mountains of rocks; and, of a similar profile, Turkey with its mosques, its wooden houses, cemeteries; Athos with monasteries closed like prisons around their single Byzantine church; Greece with temples and hovels.[2] The land was barren. It was logical for life to concentrate in the large villages. And we were not disconcerted by anything else: we knew it.[3]

Since Brindisi I have seen every style and kind of house, and every species of tree, flower, and grass! The mountains have a face. The styles are getting complicated: agglomerations often suspect.[4]

Everything leads me to single out the Turks. They were polite, solemn; they had *respect* for the presence of things. Their work is huge and beautiful, grandiose. Such unity! Such timelessness! Such wisdom! Evenings in the courtyards of great mosques.[5]

Why is our progress so ugly? Why do those whose blood is still pure hasten to take the worst from us? Do we like making art? Is it not dried up theory to go on doing it? Shall we never again create harmony?[6] The sanctuaries remain, and we will go on doubting forever.

Over there, one knows nothing of today, but only of the past; the tragic touches upon exultant joy. One's whole being is so profoundly affected because isolation is complete. It is on the Acropolis, upon the steps of the Parthenon, and over the sea beyond, that one sees the realities of long ago.[7] I am twenty years old and I cannot answer. . . .[8]

Completed at Naples on October 10, 1911, by Charles-Edouard Jeanneret. Reread on July 17, 1965, 24 rue Nungesser et Coli, by Le Corbusier.

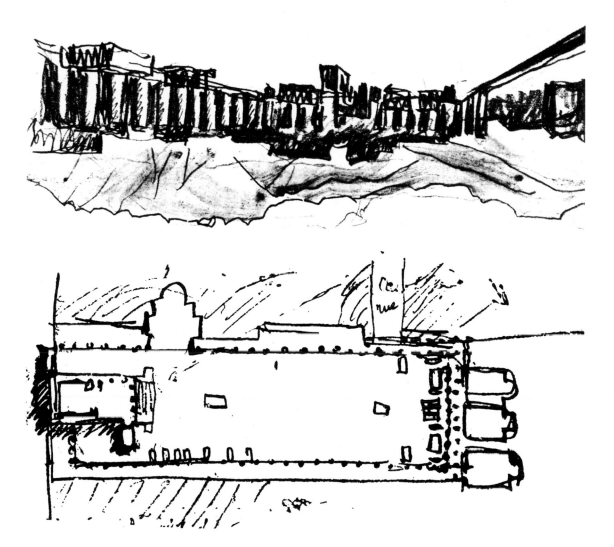

*View and plan of the
Forum in Pompeii (top,
courtesy Jean Petit;
bottom, courtesy FLC)*

*View of the Temple of Ju-
piter at the Forum in Pompeii, with Jeanneret's
reconstructed view below it
(courtesy FLC)*

*View of the Forum in Pompeii seen from the Temple of Jupiter, with columns added by Jeanneret to explain the space (courtesy FLC)*

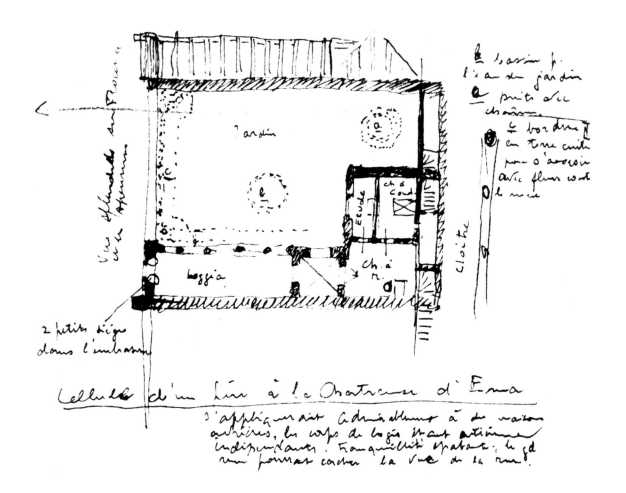

Cellules d'un Lieu à la Chartreuse d'Ema

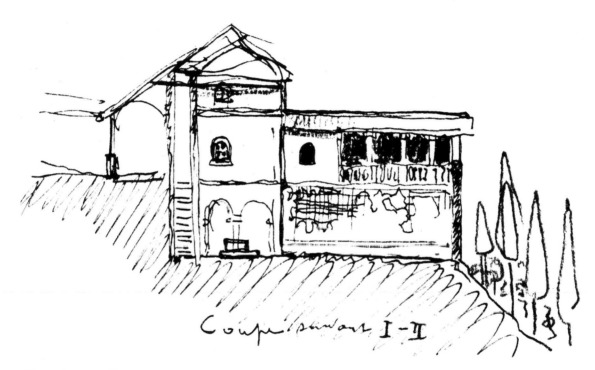

Coupe suivant I-II

Plan and cross section
through a cell of the Carthusian Monastery of Ema
(courtesy Jean Petit)

# EDITOR'S NOTES

## TO MY BROTHER, THE MUSICIAN ALBERT JEANNERET

1. Hellerau was an art colony near Dresden, Germany. Jeanneret's brother Albert was studying music at the institute there founded by Émile Jacques-Dalcroze, the Swiss composer. Later Albert Jeanneret offered courses in *Rhythmique* for adults and children in La Chaux-de-Fonds and then in Paris. In the early 1920s Albert became a regular contributor to the Jeanneret-Ozenfant journal *L'Espirit Nouveau,* writing a column on rhythm and music. He also ran a regular full-page advertisement for his course in this journal.

## A FEW IMPRESSIONS

1. In the original manuscript this chapter was entitled "En Orient—Quelques Impressions."

2. *Baedeker* was one of the few guidebooks that Jeanneret took with him on his journey to the East. While in Greece, he marked and annotated a number of passages in this book. See Paul Venable Turner, *The Education of Le Corbusier* (New York: Garland Publishing, 1977), p. 214.

3. In his correspondence with Charles L'Eplattenier, Jeanneret considered *La Sentinelle,* one of the five local newspapers of La Chaux-de-Fonds, as a possible place of publication for the installments of his travel diaries.

## A LETTER TO FRIENDS

1. In the original manuscript this chapter was entitled "Sur les Poteries Slaves."

2. The Ateliers d'Arts Reunis were the studios of the School of Art in La Chaux-de-Fonds, founded in 1910 by the former students of Le Cours Superieur de Decoration. Charles-Edouard Jeanneret, Leon Perrin, and Octave Matthey were classmates in a course taught by the director of the school,

Charles L'Eplattenier. This letter also mentions Georges Aubert and Marius Perrenond, other friends from the Ateliers d'Arts Reunis.

3. Eugene Grasset was the furniture and decorative designer whose book was used in the art school at La Chaux-de-Fonds and whom Jeanneret went to see during his stay in Paris. Grasset spoke to young Jeanneret about the complete decadence of contemporary architecture, in which he saw only one small ray of hope—the new construction method of reinforced concrete which could yield pure forms. See Paul Venable Turner, *The Education of Le Corbusier* (New York: Garland Publishing, 1977), p. 27, and Maximilien Gauthier, *Le Corbusier ou L'Architecture au Service de l'Homme* (Paris: Les Editions Denoël, 1944), p. 27.

4. Vedic refers to the language and early form of Sanskrit in which is written the Veda, an ancient collection of psalms, chants, religious mythology, and sacred formulas of Hinduism.

5. Jeanneret visited the Carthusian Monastery of Ema near Florence with his friend Leon Perrin in 1907. He returned to it for another visit toward the end of the present journey. This monastic community came to represent for him an absolute ideal of communal life, and he was later to write: "I never thought to see such a joyous interpretation of dwelling." Le Corbusier, *Precisions sur un Etat Present de l'Architecture et Urbanisme* (Paris: Vincent Freal, 1960), p. 91. See also Peter Sereyni, "Le Corbusier, Fourier, and the Monastery of Ema," *Art Bulletin* 49 (1967), pp. 277–286.

## VIENNA

1. Jean Rictus (1867–1933)—born Gabriel Randon de Saint-Armand at Boulogne-sur-Mer—was a contemporary French poet. In 1894 he wrote a number of poems, among them "L'Hiver" and "Le Revenant," in which he portrayed with a brutal, raw language the miseries and complaints of the poor. His

poems were collected in *Les Soliloques du Pauvre* (1897), *Doléances* (1900), and *Les Cantilenes du Malheur* (1902).

2. *La Feuille d'Avis,* and not *La Sentinelle,* was the newspaper in La Chaux-de-Fonds that later published Jeanneret's travel notes.

3. William Ritter (1867–1955) was a contemporary Swiss writer and art critic from Neuchâtel. He became a friend and a mentor to young Jeanneret with whom he corresponded from 1910 to 1918, while he lived in Germany and Switzerland. Through his books he influenced the itinerary Jeanneret chose and the places he visited during this journey to the East. *Leurs Lys et Leurs Roses* (1903) is a novel Ritter wrote about Vienna, its Prater and Viennese life, and which Jeanneret read, together with Ritter's *Entetement Slovaque* (1910) which centers about peasant life and popular art in Slovakia.

4. In the published 1966 text this appears as "l'unité de bien" which is a typographical error and should instead read "l'unité de lieu." This is confirmed by the original manuscript and the newspaper article which appeared in *La Feuille d'Avis* of La Chaux-de-Fonds, August 18, 1911.

5. The Schönbrunn Palace by Johann Bernard Fischer von Erlach, architect to Leopold I, was the summer palace of the Hapsburg monarchs, situated right outside of Vienna. A large, sprawling complex, it was designed in the spirit of Versailles, with elaborate interiors and a park in the French style.

6. Auguste Klipstein was at this time writing his doctoral dissertation on El Greco and going to Budapest and Bucharest to see El Greco paintings in collections there; he was later to become an art dealer in Bern. See Paul Venable Turner, *The Education of Le Corbusier* (New York: Garland Publishing, 1977), pp. 92, 213, and Maximilien Gauthier, *Le Corbusier au L'Architecture au Service de l'Homme* (Paris: Les Editions Denoël, 1944), p. 33, and letter from Jeanneret to Charles L'Eplattenier dated Cologne, May 8, 1911, now in the Bibliothèque de La Chaux-de-Fonds.

7. Jeanneret is referring to Karl-Ernst Osthaus, for whom Henri Van de Velde built the Hohenlot house between 1906 and 1907. Van de Velde also renovated the Folkwang Museum, later known as Osthaus Museum, in Hagen between 1900 and 1902.

8. Ferdinand Hodler (1853–1918), a Swiss painter, was a prominent expressionist and also a major figure in the symbolist movement. The central theme of Hodler's work is death. His father died early, and his mother remarried. Of the twelve children that made up the combined families, only six survived into maturity. *L'Elu* ("The Chosen One"), 1893–1894, is considered to be one of the more esoteric canvases dealing with the subject of birth. In this composition six women (or angels), not five as Jeanneret recalls, hover about a child kneeling before a sapling. See Robert Pinctus, "Ferdinand Hodler: Expressionism Versus Symbolism," *Artform* (March 1973), pp. 53–56.

9. Roll-Alfred Philippe (1846–1919) was a contemporary French painter, well-known for his portraits, landscapes, and military and naval scenes.

10. This was during Jeanneret's first trip to Vienna in 1907. He was accompanied by his friend and fellow student from La Chaux-de-Fonds, Leon Perrin. Jeanneret stayed there through the winter of that year, but not much is known about his activities, except that he mentions regular visits to the philharmonic concerts and the opera.

## THE DANUBE

1. The Iron Gates Bridge spanning the Danube is the best-known recorded work of public architecture under the Emperor Trajan (AD 52–117), constructed by his architect-engineer Apollodorus of Damascus. A bas-relief of this bridge can be seen in a detail depicting Trajan's Dacian victories on the Column of Trajan in Rome. See John B. Ward-Perkins, *Roman Architecture* (New York: Harry N. Abrams, 1974), pp. 119–120. Jeanneret writes about

this bridge with great enthusiasm and anticipation in a letter to Ritter dated March 1, 1911, now in the Swiss National Library in Bern.

2. At this point the following passage found in the original manuscript was omitted from the French edition: "in certain places along the river suddenly decorated with those half-loop wainscots. They are, rather, the winding rivers along the contours of the blue porcelain in the collection of Dresden."

3. Pressburg, today known as Bratislava in Czechoslovakia, lies on the northern bank of the Danube, near the Austria-Hungary border.

4. This reference is to the cathedral of Esztergom.

5. This sentence was added to the original manuscript, thus creating a confusion in verb tense in this passage.

6. In the original manuscript this sentence continues: "and this creates the most outrageous diptych imaginable, such an eyesore!"

7. In the original manuscript this paragraph continues: "Yet we ignore [the melody]. All our musical 'Sehnsucht' [longing] again dissipated under the brutal lighting of the dance halls, with their fleecy virtuosos."

8. The editor at *La Feuille d'Avis* removed the passage from "Letter to Friends" beginning with "rudely" and ending with "the horizontality of outlines."

## BUCHAREST

1. Salon d'Automne, an annual exhibition in Paris, was founded in 1903 by a group of artists that originally included the Fauves and Auguste Rodin. It came into being as a reaction against the academicism of the official salon held at Salon d'Apollon in the Louvre. The Salon d'Automne exhibitions were held at the Grand Palais, and a jury granted prizes for the works selected. The first Salon d'Automne gave Paul Gauguin a memorial exhibition in 1903, which established his reputation. Other major exhibitions followed: Paul Cézanne, the Fauves, the Cubists, Maurice Utrillo, Francis Picabia, Amedeo Modigliani,

and, of course, El Greco. Jeanneret himself first exhibited at the Salon d'Automne in 1913. His submission consisted of thirteen watercolors, eight of which were executed during the present journey.

2. Salon d'Indépendants was created in 1863 under Napoleon III as a special salon for those creative artists who were rejected by the Salon of the Royal Academy. At first it was called the Salon des Refusés, but in 1884 it changed its name to the Salon des Artistes Indépendants, in which anyone could exhibit up to two works of art once a year.

3. Philip II (1527–1598), who ruled Spain from 1556 to 1598.

4. Homaisian (homaisiennes) derives from M. Homais, the pharmacist in Flaubert's novel *Madame Bovary,* whose house is cluttered from floor to ceiling with a collection of trappings, representing to Flaubert, and Jeanneret, what must be the worst tendency of bourgeois taste during the era of Napoleon III, the Second Empire. See also Le Corbusier's mention of Homais in *L'Art Decoratif d'Aujourd'hui* (Paris, Editions Vincent, Fréal, 1925; reprinted 1959), p. 218.

5. Neither Jeanneret nor his friend Klipstein were French, and it should be assumed here that he means "since we spoke French." Jeanneret was not to become an official French citizen until nineteen years later (in September 1930), although most of his life he claimed to be French due to his origin and affinity for the Mediterranean cultures.

6. This is a reference to the École des Beaux-Arts located at the quai Voltaire on the left bank of the Seine River in Paris.

## TŬRNOVO

1. Known today as Veliko Tŭrnovo.

2. Shipka refers to the Shipka Pass in the Balkan Mountains of central Bulgaria, between Gabrovo on the north and Kazanlŭk on the south.

3. Jeanneret alludes to his earlier trip to Italy with Leon Perrin in 1907. The panels he mentions are exhibited at the Pinacoteca Nazionale in Sienna. The four separate panels depict The Triumph of Death, The Triumph of Chastity, The Triumph of Love, and The Triumph of Fame. These panels are the work of an unknown artist of the fifteenth century.

4. At this point in the original manuscript Jeanneret adds: "as it is with many villages of Valais where an already sickly race is dying out."

5. Jeanneret wrote this chapter almost two months after his actual visit to Tŭrnovo, when, as he reveals later in this discussion, he was being held in quarantine on a desert island—St. George Island in the Bay of Salamis across from Eleusis, Greece. He arrived there after he had seen Istanbul and Mount Athos.

6. Giovanni Cimabue (c. 1240–1302) was the earliest named Florentine painter whose work has survived. His work, though still in the tradition of Byzantine art, seems to have initiated the movement toward greater naturalism that began in the late thirteenth century and culminated in the Renaissance. Duccio de Buoninsegna (active 1278–1319) was the leading painter of Sienna during the early fourteenth century.

## ON TURKISH SOIL

1. In Moslem cemeteries graves are usually marked at head and foot by two tall marble tombstones on which two angels (so the Moslem believes) will seat themselves on Judgment Day to judge the soul of the deceased. (For a vivid and detailed description, see *John L. Stoddard's Lectures: Constantinople*, Vol. 2 (Chicago: George L. Shuman, 1915), pp. 66–71.)

2. Alexandre Gabriel Decamps (1803–1860), the French painter, used Near Eastern subject matter in a belated romanticism of the French school. He visited Constantinople and Asia Minor, and his *Turkish Patrol* in particular

portrays his discovery of the East, with its radiant harmonies of blue sky, sunbaked walls, details and textures of materials. Decamps, much like Jeanneret, delighted in the play of sunlight.

3. Adrianople was an ancient Turkish capital, today known as Edirne.

4. Jeanneret uses the word *pastèques* for watermelons here, but he probably means squash.

5. Pierre-Cecile Puvis de Chavanne (born in Lyon, 1824, died in Paris, 1898) is recognized as the foremost French mural painter in the second half of the nineteenth century. Among his best-known works are the large mural compositions executed In 1867 for the fine arts museum in the Palace of Longchamps in Marseille and in 1877 in the murals representing the life of Saint Geneviève in the Church of the Panthéon in Paris A retrospective memorial exhibition of his works was included in the Salon d'Automne of 1904 in Paris and in the Armory Show of 1913 in New York. *Orphée* (Orpheus) was painted in 1883; *La Mort d'Orphée* (The Death of Orpheus) in 1894.

## CONSTANTINOPLE

1. Constantinople, present-day Istanbul, is divided by water into three parts. On the European side of the Bosphorus, the Golden Horn, a narrow inlet that cuts through the city, separates Stamboul (Old Istanbul) on the south from Pera and Galata on the north. Scutari (Üsküdar) lies across the Bosphorus on the Asian side.

2. Apparently, in Pera Jeanneret and Klipstein stayed with a family by the name of Bonnal. The exact location of the Bonnal residence has not been identified.

3. In the original manuscript there follows a sentence which was omitted from the French edition: "The bottle of resin wine is almost empty."

4. Theodora (527–548), Byzantine empress and wife of Justinian I.

5. In the original manuscript the word "tortures" is used instead of "delights."

6. Jeanneret is describing the Genoese Tower, once called the Tower of Christ. Today it is popularly known as the Tower of Galata, because it dominates the Galata quarter of Pera. In 1350 the tower was surmounted by the cross of Genoa. It has been used as a post for firewatchers and, most recently, as a restaurant and night club.

7. In the original manuscript the word "bestial" is used instead of "brutal."

8. The word "coarse" is deleted before "sea merchants" in the original manuscript.

9. In the original manuscript the word "squandering" is used to qualify "offices."

10. In the original manuscript the word "Greek" is used in place of "merchant." Le Corbusier in his emendations of the text in 1965 seems to have had second thoughts about national stereotyping.

11. Imam is a title given to a Moslem prayer leader, or, more generally, to any of various Moslems who have authority in matters of theology and law.

## THE MOSQUES

1. Pierre Loti (1850–1923), a French novelist, was a naval officer during the French occupation of Istanbul.

2. Jeanneret is describing the Mosque of Suleyman.

3. It is odd that Jeanneret mentions plane trees here because according to Turkish custom cypress trees, not plane trees, were planted beside each newly made grave.

4. Old fortifications at the outskirts of the city whose foundations are said to have been laid by Constantine himself.

5. The Sultan Mehmet, also known as the Fatih Mosque or Mosque of the Conqueror, was built by Sultan Mehmet in the form of a complex that includes several important tombs.

6. He is referring to the Aqueduct of Valens.

7. The Mosque of Prince Shehzade was built in 1548 as a memorial to a favorite son of the sultan, who had died in 1543.

8. The Mosque of Suleyman (also called Sulemaniye) was the third and the noblest mosque built for the Sultan Suleyman by Sinan. The mosque itself is the center of an extensive group of ancillary buildings, including four schools, a training college, a library, a bath, a hospital, a public kitchen to feed worshippers, and a hostel to lodge them. See Michael Maclagen, *The City of Constantinople* (New York: Frederic A. Praeger, 1968), pp. 135–136.

9. The Beyazit Mosque is named after Sultan Bayazit II (1481–1512). It was the first of the great imperial mosques built between 1501 and 1505 on the forum of Theodosius. Nuruosmaniye (Light of Osman) is not known as the Mosque of the Tulips (Mosque of Laleli). The latter was probably called that for its flowerlike beauty, for it was not erected until long after the reign of the Tulip Prince, Ahmet III. See Robert Lidell, *Byzantium and Istanbul* (London: Jonathan Cape, 1956) p. 179.

10. This dilapidated column, blackened by fire and kept from disintegration by a series of iron rings, has been standing for over fifteen centuries. On its top was placed the famous bronze statue of Apollo by Phidias. See *John L. Stoddard's Lectures: Constantinople*, Vol. 2 (Chicago: George L. Shuman, 1915), p. 38.

11. The Mosque of Mihrimah Pasha was built for the Princess Mihrimah, daughter of Suleyman the Magnificent and wife of Rustem Pasha.

12. In Turkish cemeteries a tombstone denoting the grave of a man is always crowned with a turban or a fez, carved in marble. Over the years many of

these tombstones have fallen to the ground, leaving the turbans strewn about like decapitated heads.

## THE SEPULCHERS

1. The theorbos is a type of lute, now obsolete, with a double neck and two sets of strings.

2. In the original manuscript the phrase "comme autrefois, ceux des 'Cent-Suisses'" ("like in the old days would the 'Hundred Swiss'") is added here. The "Cent-Suisse" refers to a company of mercenary soldiers that served in various European armies. Swiss mercenaries were particularly numerous in the Royal French armies under the Ancien Regime. When these expatriated soldiers would hear melodies recalling the horns or shepherd songs of their native land, nostalgia would overcome them just as it has at this point the young Jeanneret.

3. For the sake of clarity, a phrase from the original manuscript omitted in the French publication has been reinstated here: "they mount the hill, then facing the sea."

4. Ayvan Saray ("The Great Palace") is the site of the old imperial wharf on the north side of the Golden Horn. Topkapu ("Cannon Gate," or the gate of St. Romanus) is one of the principal entrances into the city through the old walls from the west side.

5. At this point the original manuscript continues: "Et c'est comme si je les voyais,—les 'Heures Tristes,' accrochées dans Saint-Pol-Roux, ou donjon de Divine." ("And it is as if I could see them, the 'cheerless hours' suspended in Saint-Pol-Roux, from the dungeon of the Divine.") Saint-Pol-Roux (1861–1940) was a French symbolist poet who wrote a tragic poem entitled "La Dame à la Faulx" (1899), rich in images and allegories, that Jeanneret is alluding to at this point. Other symbolic poets, such as Stéphane Mallarmé and Villiers de L'Isle-Adam, not only influenced Saint-Pol-Roux but were

greatly admired by the small circle of artists and poets of La Chaux-de-Fonds of which Jeanneret was a member.

6. Eyüp is a holy place and a favorite burial ground for sultans and viziers.

## SHE'S AND HE'S

1. Jeanneret means women and donkeys, and not women and men.

2. The sentence, "It's inconsistent to say something like this," follows in the original manuscript.

3. Musée Guimet is located in Paris. Its founder, Émile-Étienne Guimet (1836–1918), amassed a collection of religious art from India, China, and Japan. The phrase "at any price because it is so powerful" appears next in the original manuscript.

4. Beykoz is a village northeast of Istanbul on the Asian side of the Bosphorus.

5. Theophile Gautier (1811–1872) was a French poet and critic. Tarabya is a small resort town on the European side of the Bosphorus, just north of Istanbul, often associated with the last years of the Ottoman Empire.

6. The recipients of these cards were his friend Leon Perrin and Madame L'Eplattenier, the wife of his mentor. To my knowledge, it was the first card during this journey that Jeanneret wrote to Madame L'Eplattenier, and in it he writes: "Here one does not touch lightly upon the subject of women. But just yesterday (I confessed this to Perrin) a young Turkish girl, so exquisite I'd say (though it makes me bite my tongue), one à la Loti, spoke to me. Then all the walls caved in, and here I am sending greetings to all women—friendly, adoring, loving, ecstatic, and who knows? And here is my proof. Affectionately yours, Ch.-Ed. Jeanneret."

7. In the original manuscript Jeanneret writes, and then crosses out, a whole final paragraph in which he compares the donkeys from Stamboul with those of a certain Mr. Reymond in La Chaux-de-Fonds. He probably considered this

passage either too personal or too parochial, and thus omitted it from this chapter. The Mr. Reymond mentioned here by Jeanneret was a lively local character whom the old inhabitants of La Chaux-de-Fonds remember to this day. He was a small merchant who made home deliveries in a cart pulled by a donkey.

## A CAFÉ

1. The phrase "or are absorbed in a doleful 'kef'" followed in the original manuscript.

2. In the original manuscript the last part of the sentence reads: "a lantern hung to some tree which had sprouted there burns every night to illuminate the tombstone whose worn inscriptions, *as beautiful as golden arabesques against a black background,* no doubt recall under the delicate guise of an Eastern allegory the virtues of brave men now resting between the roots of the great sycamore which rises like their soul to heaven and which every year drops its fruit to earth again."

3. Here the original manuscript includes another sentence: "[The fruit] evokes for [the old people] a bright, iridescent rainbow even more brilliant than that which emanates from the domes, into which the minarets dissolve."

## SESAME

1. Kutahya is a Turkish city southeast of Istanbul in Anatolia.

2. Porrentruy is a city in northwestern Switzerland.

3. Jeanneret is using the metaphor "Open, Sesame!" from the legendary story of "Ali Baba and the Forty Thieves" in *One Thousand and One Arabian Nights.*

4. The phrase "the cool smile of a German after a victory" was omitted in the French edition.

## TWO FANTASIES, ONE REALITY

1. Dolmabahçe is the largest and most imposing of all the sultan's palaces, a sort of imperial village more than a third of a mile long, constructed by Sultan Abdul Mejid along the Bosphorus on the European side. It was burned down in 1908 (three years before Jeanneret's visit), just after the ascension of Mohammed V, when the Young Turk party overthrew the sultan.

2. The Mosque of Rustem Pasha, designed by the great architect Sinan in 1561, is especially well known for its elegant ceramic tile work, which is considered among the best of the period. It is located near the Galata Bridge, not far from the New Mosque.

3. Hamals are Turkish porters.

## THE STAMBOUL DISASTER

1. Denis-August-Marie Raffet (1804–1860) was a French painter whose lithographs often portrayed the soldiers of the French Revolution and Napoleon's Old Guard. Jena, Germany, is chiefly known to the French because it is near the battleground where Napoleon defeated the Prussians in 1806. The mural Jeanneret is referring to depicts "The Battle of Jena," painted by Horace Vernet (1789–1863); it hangs in Versailles.

2. Validé Mosque, better known as Yeni Validé or Yeni Cami ("New Mosque"), stands on the square at the south end of the Galata Bridge. Construction began in 1597 but was interrupted several times before its completion in 1663.

3. "Veni Capon" appears in the 1966 French edition, but it is "Yeni Capou" in the original typed manuscript. Probably what was intended here is "Yeni Cami" near the Galata Bridge or Azap Kapu at the new Atatürk Bridge.

4. The original manuscript concludes with the following paragraph: "Beneath our windows the 'Young Turks' from Pera celebrate Constitution Day. The Greek population sneers, seeing the Turk roasting over there beyond the Golden Horn, in his Stamboul amid his mosques whose minarets lift their useless arms up to the sky and whose domes bury one more secret under the oppression of their suffocating cupolas.—Pera, July 24, 1911, Ch.-Ed. Jeanneret."

## A JUMBLE OF RECOLLECTIONS AND REGRETS

1. The term *Paradis* ("Paradise") appears in the 1966 French edition, but the original manuscript reads *Paraclis* ("Paraclete, or the Holy Spirit"). Jeanneret had visited and was very impressed with the Chapel of Paraclis in Bucharest—so much so that he mentioned it enthusiastically in two letters to William Ritter (June 3 and July 6, 1911), now in the Swiss National Library in Bern.

2. Jacob Jordaens (1593–1678) of Antwerp, Adriaen Brouwer (1606–1638), born in Oudenaarde, and Andrien Van Ostäde (1610–1685), active in Haarlem, born in Lübeck, were genre painters known for pictures that depict rollicking peasants at feasts or peasants carousing or brawling in taverns and barns.

3. Gascon refers to an inhabitant of the province of Gascogne in southern France, near the Spanish border. People from this region are known for their exuberance and boasting.

4. Batum is a seaport on the Black Sea in Georgia (USSR) that was active in the oil trade at the time of Jeanneret's journey to the East.

5. A caïque is a light wooden rowboat used on the Bosphorus.

6. The French term *Pathé* refers to the brand name of a phonograph invented by Guglielmo Marconi (1874–1937). *La Voix de Son Maître* is the company's trademark.

7. A firman is a decree enforced by authorities in the East.

8. Philippolis, now called Plovdiv, is a city on the Maritsa River, in southern Bulgaria.

9. Heliopolis was the name of both an ancient ruined city south of Cairo and the Arabic city of Masr-el-Gedida, a suburb northeast of Cairo, which is the city Jeanneret has in mind.

10. In Cairo a *moucharaby,* or moucharabieh, is a wooden lattice screen placed around the perimeter of a projecting window opening to the street, through which one can see without being seen.

## RECOLLECTIONS OF ATHOS

1. Xiropotamou is one of the twenty monasteries on Mount Athos.

2. Karies is the administrative and religious center of the community of Mount Athos. Here a visitor would stop to be issued a *diamonitirion* (a permit), which authorizes him to visit the Holy Mountain.

3. Jeanneret is referring to the details of one of the frescoes by Benozzo Gozzoli (1400–1497), entitled "The Intoxication of Noah," on the walls of the Camposanto at Pisa, which he probably saw on his trip to Italy in 1907.

4. Jeanneret is describing a painting by Jean-Antoine Watteau (1684–1721), "Departure from the Island of Cytherea," which depicts a pilgrimage of lovers setting out from the Island of Cytherea, the idyllic land of love and happiness, with the sea and misty horizons before them. A marquis and a marquise occupy the central position, somewhat detached from the rest of the group and seen from the back.

5. There are in fact twenty monasteries on Mount Athos: Zografou, Konstamonitou, Dohiariou, Xenofontos, St. Panteleimon or Rossikon, Xiropotamou, Simonos Petras, Ossiou Grigoriou, St. Dionissiou, St. Pavlou, Esfigmenou, Hiliandariou, Vatopediou, Pantokratoros, Stavronikita, Koutloumoussiou, Iviron, Filotheou, Karakallou, and Megistis Lavras. Their number is fixed at

twenty, and according to the state charter of Mount Athos no additional monastery may be founded on the peninsula. Besides these twenty monasteries there are twelve sketes, communities composed of several buildings centered around a church similar, but subordinate, to the monasteries. Different regions, such as Russia, Bulgaria, and Serbia, are represented by different monasteries and sketes. The peninsula also contains a number of hermitages, small grottos, and refuges of peace and tranquility often consisting of only a single room.

6. The Monastery of Iviron.

7. Prodromos is not a monastery but a Rumanian skete.

8. The word "salamanders" might be used figuratively here to characterize the working monks who can enjoy, as well as endure, the extreme heat.

9. Since 1907 the Triple Entente of England, France, and Russia had been poised against Germany, Austro-Hungary, and Italy.

10. Rossikon is a monastery also known at St. Panteleimon.

11. Isidore of Miletus and Anthemius of Tralles were the architects of Hagia Sophia.

12. The peninsula of Chalkidiki is located between the Gulf of Salonika and the Strymonic Gulf (Gulf of Strimon).

13. The prince could have been Serbian or Bulgarian but not Croatian, since most Croatians are Roman Catholics, not Eastern Orthodox. There is also no indication that Croatians ever built a monastery or skete on Mount Athos.

14. The Sassanian refers to the Sassanid dynasty in Persia, which lasted from the third to the seventh centuries, A.D.

15. This reference is to Jeanneret's 1907 trip to Italy at which time he visited St. Appolinaire in Classe.

16. According to ancient tradition, the monasteries of Mount Athos lock their doors at sunset to prevent evil spirits from entering. The belief persists, even to this day, that some of the monasteries and sketes are haunted by demons.

17. Mount Athos is governed by delegates called *epistates.* Every year at the end of May, each of the twenty monasteries sends one representative, or epistate, to a governing body for a one-year term. The *protos* is a sort of general governor of Mount Athos, elected by the epistates.
In Wagner's *Parsifal,* Amfortas is the keeper of the Holy Grail who suffers from a lingering wound that makes it possible for him to resist Kundry's embraces in Act II, Scene 2.

18. A regulation dating from the eleventh century, but still in effect, prohibits any woman, female animal, eunuch, or even anyone with a smooth face from having access to Mount Athos. It also prohibits the products of female animals, such as milk, butter, cheese, and eggs.

## THE PARTHENON

1. The original manuscript adds here: "the most tyrannical of laws."

2. The original manuscript adds here: "the tyrant, the dictator."

3. A sentence from the original manuscript is omitted here: "Willowy as a maiden and encircled by an entablature so smooth and limpid that it reminds you of absolutely clear, fresh water in fine crystal."

4. The original manuscript adds here: "following the layer from which it was extracted from Mount Pentelicus."

5. The following sentences from the original manuscript are omitted here: "What speculation about the metaphysics of marble! Demeter and the Parcae, the Illisus and Theseus, are for us a language more readily expressed in an organic form, at best articulated by torsoes and heads, glances and foreheads."

6. Although the word *colline* ("hill") appears in the book version, the word *carene* ("hull") appears in the original manuscript, and is restored here.

7. The following sentence from the original manuscript is omitted here: "One cannot listen to this without feeling contempt, or in some way sad—it is as lamentable as that autumn in Versailles."

8. At this point in the original manuscript Jeanneret continues: "All the ugliness of customs accosts us, all residuals of a dying religion; I would rather not speak here of those who live in this most beautiful city at the very foot of the temples; besides, they are not in the least related to the ancient races and great builders; they are what they are. I have not examined them at all, being too distracted by *the other*. The other, the great temple in its boundless light."

9. Jeanneret is referring to the Carthusian Monastery at Galluzzo on the Ema, just south of Florence, which he first visited in 1907. It made an indelible impression on him at that time, so much so that he returned to it once again toward the end of the present journey to sketch it.

10. Jeanneret makes five attempts in 1914 to conclude the chapter here. The first attempt was published in the 1966 French edition. In a second, he ends with the question. "Suggestions?" This question was probably addressed to William Ritter, to whom the manuscript was mailed for possible publication. In a third attempt, Jeanneret describes the ruins of the Parthenon in terms of the heroic, fallen warriors of a Homeric epic. From this passage comes the final paragraph of the chapter, as published. The fourth attempt was the paragraph: "My message is dignified, for the swinging ship that carries me between the tranquil Achaia and then the Peloponnesus is charged by a thunderstorm, so I can no longer think of anything but the smooth front of the temple, which is naked, thank God, and bereft of all coloration, vanquished, plundered by man yet the master of all time. The Acropolis, the precipitous pedestal of the full imagination. The Parthenon, the standard for all creation!"

The final attempt reads: "My message is dignified, filled with the mirth of carrying with it the imperishable image of the temple."

## IN THE WEST

1. As the final chapter of the original 1911 manuscript, this chapter followed "A Jumble of Recollections and Regrets." About half of it, however, was omitted in the French edition.

2. Omitted here from the original manuscript is the sentence: "The temple has a few columns and an entablature."

3. "It was a unitary transcendent principle" is omitted here from the original manuscript.

4. "Agglomerations often suspect" reads in the original manuscript: "With agglomerations that are often ugly, awful, disgusting. Church interiors are horrible, the paintings, too. People in the streets shout and have no manners."

5. The original text suppressed here continues with a new paragraph:
*Alas, why is this disintegrating? Collapsing everywhere. Integrity is completely lost; the filth increases. Where will there still be decent practice, where is there any? Everywhere horrors affront its very essence. Ingenuousness is discredited and withdraws. Progress becomes Attilian. What an awful leveling will there be then? Theoretically, this would lead to a more judicious and dignified unity. Would it not?*
*The Japanese wear the monocle, while the stones of the pagoda are abandoned to oblivion in the jungle. Madame de Staël would no longer desire to die after seeing the Naples of today. The Parthenon is dead; it is a ghost over there that crushes to the end. Technology has killed Philae, alcohol the negroes, and religion has clothed their beautiful naked forms. Nothing original remains any longer.*

6. Another paragraph is omitted here: "Is it necessary to include everyone when creating, or is it less idiotic, more honest, to think only about oneself?

Do Piero della Francesca and César Franck need to be known by the masses? Do the masses need them?"

7. At this point the original manuscript is dated, "Pompeii, October 8, 1911," but it continues with one more short paragraph, an epilogue in the form of a confession:

*I have finished at last! Why have I undertaken this fruitless task? I wanted "to commit myself," to be obliged to pursue it to the very end. I thought it would be nice to have living memories of this journey. These notes are lifeless; the beauties I have seen always break down under my pen; there were murderous repetitions. That would bore me and torment me for hours, disheartening hours of vexation, of despair. Often that deprived me of the serenity to which so many lines had enticed me while across blue seas as calm as mirrors we sailed unaware in the ineffable light and under the moon. During my hours of gold, ivory, and crystal, there were flaws, stains, and cracks—because of these notes that I so wanted to write! I didn't know my own language, I have never studied it! I can still hear the tol-de-rol of the four or five adjectives I know. And that noise of a huge bass drum dissipated by the wind reminds me of those tedious dominical afternoons, whenever there is a kermis not far away—a kermis in La Chaux-de-Fonds. O Breughel! Completed at Naples this October 10, 1911. Ch-Ed. Jeanneret*

8. Le Corbusier added this final sentence in 1965.

# LIST OF DRAWINGS

*All drawings date from 1911.*

This book was set in VIP Gill Sans by DEKR Corporation and printed and bound by Halliday Lithograph in the United States of America.

Library of Congress Cataloging-in-Publication Data

Le Corbusier, 1887–1965.
Journey to the East.

Translation of: Le Voyage d'Orient.
1. Architecture—Europe. 2. Architecture—Turkey—Istanbul. 3. Istanbul (Turkey)—Buildings, structures, etc. 4. Le Corbusier, 1887–1965—Journeys—Europe. 5. Le Corbusier, 1887–1965—Journeys—Turkey—Istanbul. 6. Le Corbusier, 1887–1965—Diaries. 7. Architects—France—Diaries. I. Žaknić, Ivan. II. Title.
NA950.L4V613 1987        720′.92′4 [B]        86-20886
ISBN 0-262-12091-7